50 Melon Recipes for Home

By: Kelly Johnson

Table of Contents

- Melon Salad with Feta and Mint
- Melon Gazpacho
- Grilled Melon Skewers
- Melon Prosciutto Wraps
- Melon Sorbet
- Melon Agua Fresca
- Melon and Cucumber Salsa
- Melon Caprese Salad
- Melon Smoothie Bowl
- Melon Fruit Salad
- Melon and Prosciutto Pizza
- Melon Granita
- Melon Ceviche
- Melon Mint Lemonade
- Melon Sangria
- Melon Bruschetta
- Melon Popsicles
- Melon and Shrimp Salad
- Melon Stuffed with Chicken Salad
- Melon Margarita
- Melon and Avocado Salad
- Melon Panzanella
- Melon Tuna Poke Bowl
- Melon and Cucumber Gazpacho
- Melon and Mint Infused Water
- Melon Jelly
- Melon Yogurt Parfait
- Melon and Goat Cheese Crostini
- Melon Chutney
- Melon Mousse
- Melon and Basil Salad
- Melon Brulee
- Melon Teriyaki Chicken Skewers
- Melon Coconut Rice Pudding
- Melon Margherita Pizza

- Melon and Crab Salad
- Melon and Prosciutto Pasta
- Melon Panna Cotta
- Melon and Feta Bruschetta
- Melon and Mint Sorbet Float
- Melon Cucumber Rolls
- Melon and Pork Stir-Fry
- Melon and Brie Quesadillas
- Melon and Blueberry Crisp
- Melon and Basil Lemonade
- Melon and Cilantro Rice
- Melon and Ricotta Toast
- Melon Breakfast Smoothie
- Melon and Chicken Lettuce Wraps
- Melon Slaw

Melon Salad with Feta and Mint

Ingredients:

- 1 small seedless watermelon, cubed
- 1 small honeydew melon, cubed
- 200g feta cheese, crumbled
- Fresh mint leaves, chopped
- 2 tablespoons extra virgin olive oil
- Juice of 1 lime or lemon
- Salt and black pepper, to taste

Instructions:

Prepare the Melons:
- Cut the watermelon and honeydew melon into bite-sized cubes. Remove any seeds or rind.

Assemble the Salad:
- In a large serving bowl, combine the cubed watermelon and honeydew melon.

Add the Feta and Mint:
- Sprinkle the crumbled feta cheese over the melon cubes.
- Chop the fresh mint leaves and scatter them over the salad.

Dress the Salad:
- In a small bowl, whisk together the olive oil and lime or lemon juice.
- Drizzle the dressing over the salad.

Season and Toss:
- Gently toss the salad to combine all the ingredients.
- Season with salt and black pepper according to your taste.

Chill and Serve:
- Place the salad in the refrigerator to chill for about 30 minutes before serving.
- Garnish with extra mint leaves if desired.

Tips:

- For variation, you can substitute other types of melons like cantaloupe or Crenshaw melon.
- Adjust the amount of feta cheese and mint based on your preference.

- This salad pairs well with grilled meats or as a refreshing side dish for summer gatherings.

Enjoy your Melon Salad with Feta and Mint!

Melon Gazpacho

Ingredients:

- 1 small seedless watermelon, peeled and cubed
- 1 small cantaloupe melon, peeled and cubed
- 1 cucumber, peeled, seeded, and diced
- 1 red bell pepper, seeded and diced
- 1 small red onion, diced
- 2-3 cloves garlic, minced
- 3 tablespoons red wine vinegar
- 1/4 cup extra virgin olive oil
- Salt and black pepper, to taste
- Fresh basil or mint leaves, for garnish

Instructions:

Prepare the Ingredients:
- In a large bowl, combine the cubed watermelon, cantaloupe, diced cucumber, red bell pepper, red onion, and minced garlic.

Blend the Soup:
- Working in batches if necessary, transfer some of the mixed ingredients into a blender.
- Add a portion of the red wine vinegar, olive oil, salt, and black pepper to the blender.
- Blend until smooth. Adjust the consistency by adding more watermelon juice or water if it's too thick.

Combine and Chill:
- Pour the blended mixture into a large bowl or container.
- Stir well to combine all the batches.
- Taste and adjust seasoning as needed.

Chill and Serve:
- Cover the gazpacho and refrigerate for at least 2 hours or until thoroughly chilled.

Garnish and Serve:
- Before serving, taste the gazpacho again and adjust seasoning if necessary.
- Ladle the chilled gazpacho into bowls or glasses.
- Garnish with fresh basil or mint leaves.

Tips:

- You can adjust the ingredients based on your taste preferences. Some variations include adding a splash of lime juice or a hint of chili for extra zest.
- Serve the gazpacho with crusty bread or croutons for a more substantial meal.
- This soup can be made ahead of time and stored in the refrigerator for a day or two.

Enjoy your Melon Gazpacho as a light and cooling dish during warm weather!

Grilled Melon Skewers

Ingredients:

- 1 small seedless watermelon
- 1 small honeydew melon
- 1 small cantaloupe melon
- Wooden or metal skewers
- Olive oil, for brushing
- Honey, for drizzling (optional)
- Fresh mint leaves, for garnish

Instructions:

Prepare the Melons:
- Cut the watermelon, honeydew melon, and cantaloupe into bite-sized cubes or balls.

Assemble the Skewers:
- Thread the melon pieces onto skewers, alternating between the different types of melon to create colorful patterns.

Preheat the Grill:
- Preheat your grill to medium-high heat.

Grill the Skewers:
- Lightly brush the melon skewers with olive oil to prevent sticking.
- Place the skewers on the preheated grill and cook for 2-3 minutes per side, or until grill marks form and the melon begins to caramelize slightly.
- Turn the skewers carefully using tongs to grill all sides evenly.

Serve:
- Once grilled, transfer the skewers to a serving platter.
- Optionally, drizzle the grilled melon skewers with a little honey for added sweetness.
- Garnish with fresh mint leaves.

Enjoy:
- Serve the grilled melon skewers immediately while still warm.
- They can be enjoyed as a light and unique appetizer or dessert.

Tips:

- If using wooden skewers, soak them in water for about 30 minutes before threading the melon to prevent burning on the grill.

- You can customize this recipe by adding a sprinkle of salt, chili powder, or a squeeze of lime juice for a savory and tangy twist.
- Experiment with different types of melon or add other fruits like strawberries or pineapple to the skewers for more variety.

Grilled Melon Skewers are a delightful way to enjoy melons in a new and exciting way.

They're perfect for summer gatherings or backyard barbecues!

Melon Prosciutto Wraps

Ingredients:

- 1 small seedless watermelon or cantaloupe
- 8-10 slices of prosciutto
- Fresh basil leaves
- Balsamic glaze (optional)
- Toothpicks or small skewers

Instructions:

Prepare the Melon:
- Cut the seedless watermelon or cantaloupe into small cubes or wedges. Ensure they are bite-sized for wrapping.

Assemble the Wraps:
- Take a slice of prosciutto and lay it flat on a clean surface.
- Place a basil leaf on top of the prosciutto slice.
- Add a piece of melon (watermelon or cantaloupe) on top of the basil leaf.

Roll and Secure:
- Carefully roll the prosciutto slice around the melon and basil leaf, ensuring it's tightly wrapped.
- Secure the wrap with a toothpick or small skewer to hold it in place.

Repeat:
- Continue assembling the melon prosciutto wraps until all ingredients are used.

Serve:
- Arrange the wraps on a serving platter.
- Optionally, drizzle some balsamic glaze over the wraps for added flavor and presentation.

Enjoy:
- Serve the melon prosciutto wraps immediately as a delightful appetizer or party snack.

Tips:

- Choose ripe and sweet melons for the best flavor.
- Feel free to experiment with different herbs like mint or arugula instead of basil.
- Add a sprinkle of freshly ground black pepper or a squeeze of lemon juice for extra zest.

- These wraps can be prepared ahead of time and refrigerated until ready to serve.

Melon Prosciutto Wraps are perfect for summer gatherings, brunches, or any occasion where you want to impress with a simple yet elegant appetizer. Enjoy!

Melon Sorbet

Ingredients:

- 1 small seedless watermelon or cantaloupe (about 4 cups of cubed melon)
- 1/2 cup granulated sugar (adjust based on sweetness of melon)
- 1/4 cup water
- Juice of 1 lemon or lime

Instructions:

Prepare the Melon:
- Cut the seedless watermelon or cantaloupe into small cubes, discarding any seeds and rind.
- You'll need about 4 cups of cubed melon for this recipe.

Make Simple Syrup:
- In a small saucepan, combine the granulated sugar and water over medium heat.
- Stir until the sugar is completely dissolved, creating a simple syrup.
- Remove from heat and let it cool to room temperature.

Blend the Sorbet Base:
- In a blender or food processor, combine the cubed melon, cooled simple syrup, and fresh lemon or lime juice.
- Blend until smooth and well combined.

Chill the Mixture:
- Transfer the blended mixture into a shallow container or bowl.
- Cover and refrigerate for at least 2 hours, or until thoroughly chilled.

Churn the Sorbet:
- Pour the chilled sorbet mixture into an ice cream maker.
- Churn according to the manufacturer's instructions until the mixture reaches a slushy, frozen consistency (typically about 20-25 minutes).

Serve or Freeze:
- Transfer the churned sorbet into an airtight container.
- Freeze for an additional 2-3 hours or until firm.

Enjoy:
- Scoop the melon sorbet into bowls or cones.
- Garnish with fresh mint leaves or melon balls if desired.
- Serve and enjoy this refreshing homemade treat!

Tips:

- If you don't have an ice cream maker, you can still make sorbet by pouring the chilled mixture into a shallow pan. Place it in the freezer and stir every 30 minutes until it reaches the desired consistency.
- Adjust the sweetness of the sorbet by adding more or less sugar based on the natural sweetness of the melon.
- Experiment with different types of melons or add a splash of flavored liqueur (such as melon liqueur) for extra depth of flavor.

Homemade Melon Sorbet is a delightful and healthy dessert option that's perfect for cooling off on hot days. Enjoy the fresh taste of melons in every spoonful!

Melon Agua Fresca

Ingredients:

- 4 cups cubed seedless watermelon or cantaloupe
- 2 cups cold water
- Juice of 2 limes
- 2-4 tablespoons granulated sugar, honey, or agave syrup (adjust to taste)
- Ice cubes, for serving
- Fresh mint leaves or lime slices, for garnish (optional)

Instructions:

Prepare the Melon:
- Cut the seedless watermelon or cantaloupe into small cubes, removing any seeds and rind.

Blend the Melon:
- In a blender, combine the cubed melon, cold water, lime juice, and sweetener of your choice (sugar, honey, or agave syrup).
- Blend until smooth and well combined.

Strain (Optional):
- For a smoother consistency, you can strain the blended mixture through a fine mesh sieve to remove any pulp. This step is optional depending on your preference.

Chill:
- Transfer the agua fresca to a pitcher and refrigerate until thoroughly chilled, about 1-2 hours.

Serve:
- Fill glasses with ice cubes.
- Stir the chilled melon agua fresca and pour into the prepared glasses.

Garnish:
- Garnish with fresh mint leaves or lime slices for an extra touch of flavor and presentation.

Enjoy:
- Serve immediately and enjoy this refreshing melon agua fresca on a hot day!

Tips:

- Feel free to customize this recipe by using different varieties of melon or adding other fruits like strawberries or cucumbers for additional flavor.
- Adjust the sweetness level to your liking. Start with less sweetener and add more as needed.
- This agua fresca can be made ahead of time and stored in the refrigerator for up to 1-2 days.
- If you prefer a fizzy version, you can add a splash of sparkling water or soda just before serving.

Melon Agua Fresca is a light and hydrating beverage that's perfect for picnics, parties, or simply as a refreshing drink to enjoy throughout the day. Cheers to a taste of summer with this delightful melon drink!

Melon and Cucumber Salsa

Ingredients:

- 1 cup diced seedless watermelon
- 1 cup diced cucumber (English cucumber works well)
- 1/2 cup diced red onion
- 1 jalapeño pepper, seeded and finely chopped (adjust to taste)
- 1/4 cup chopped fresh cilantro or mint leaves
- Juice of 1 lime
- Salt and pepper, to taste

Instructions:

Prepare the Ingredients:
- Dice the seedless watermelon, cucumber, red onion, and jalapeño pepper. Chop the fresh cilantro or mint leaves.

Combine Ingredients:
- In a medium bowl, combine the diced watermelon, cucumber, red onion, jalapeño pepper, and chopped cilantro or mint.

Add Lime Juice and Seasoning:
- Squeeze the juice of one lime over the salsa.
- Season with salt and pepper, to taste.

Mix Well:
- Gently toss all the ingredients together until well combined.

Chill (Optional):
- For best flavor, cover the salsa and refrigerate for about 30 minutes to allow the flavors to meld together.

Serve:
- Serve the melon and cucumber salsa as a refreshing appetizer or side dish.
- Enjoy with tortilla chips, grilled meats, seafood, or as a topping for tacos and salads.

Tips:

- Customize the salsa by adding diced avocado or mango for extra creaminess or sweetness.
- Adjust the level of spiciness by adding more or less jalapeño pepper, or leave the seeds in for a hotter salsa.

- If you prefer a sweeter salsa, you can drizzle a little honey or agave syrup over the mixture before tossing.
- This salsa is best enjoyed fresh but can be stored in the refrigerator for up to 2 days.

Melon and cucumber salsa is perfect for summer gatherings, BBQs, or any occasion where you want to serve a vibrant and unique salsa. It's light, refreshing, and bursting with flavor!

Melon Caprese Salad

Ingredients:

- 1 small seedless watermelon or cantaloupe
- 8 ounces fresh mozzarella cheese, sliced
- Fresh basil leaves
- Balsamic glaze or reduction
- Extra virgin olive oil
- Salt and pepper, to taste

Instructions:

Prepare the Melon and Cheese:
- Cut the seedless watermelon or cantaloupe into thin slices or cubes.
- Slice the fresh mozzarella cheese into similar-sized slices.

Assemble the Salad:
- On a serving platter or individual plates, arrange alternating layers of melon slices or cubes with mozzarella slices.
- Tuck fresh basil leaves between the melon and cheese.

Drizzle with Olive Oil:
- Drizzle extra virgin olive oil over the melon and mozzarella.
- Season lightly with salt and pepper.

Finish with Balsamic Glaze:
- Drizzle balsamic glaze or reduction over the salad for a tangy sweetness. You can use store-bought balsamic glaze or make your own by reducing balsamic vinegar until thickened.

Garnish and Serve:
- Garnish the salad with additional fresh basil leaves.
- Serve immediately as a refreshing appetizer or side dish.

Tips:

- For added flavor and texture, you can sprinkle the salad with toasted pine nuts or chopped pistachios.
- If you prefer a savory twist, add a few slices of prosciutto or crispy pancetta to the salad.
- Try using different varieties of melon for a colorful and unique presentation.
- Adjust the amount of balsamic glaze based on your preference for sweetness and acidity.

This Melon Caprese Salad is perfect for summer gatherings, brunches, or as a light and elegant starter for any meal. Enjoy the combination of sweet melon, creamy mozzarella, and fresh basil with a drizzle of balsamic glaze!

Melon Smoothie Bowl

Ingredients:

- 2 cups cubed seedless watermelon or cantaloupe
- 1 frozen banana, sliced
- 1/2 cup plain Greek yogurt (or dairy-free alternative for vegan option)
- 1 tablespoon honey or maple syrup (optional, adjust to taste)
- Toppings (such as sliced fresh fruits, granola, nuts, seeds, coconut flakes, or mint leaves)

Instructions:

Prepare the Ingredients:
- Cut the seedless watermelon or cantaloupe into small cubes. Freeze the banana slices in advance.

Blend the Smoothie Base:
- In a blender, combine the cubed melon, frozen banana slices, Greek yogurt, and honey or maple syrup (if using).
- Blend until smooth and creamy. Add a splash of water or juice if needed to reach desired consistency.

Assemble the Smoothie Bowl:
- Pour the smoothie mixture into a bowl.

Add Toppings:
- Arrange your favorite toppings over the smoothie bowl. Some popular choices include sliced fresh fruits (berries, kiwi, banana), granola, nuts (almonds, walnuts), seeds (chia seeds, pumpkin seeds), coconut flakes, and fresh mint leaves.

Serve and Enjoy:
- Serve the melon smoothie bowl immediately and enjoy with a spoon.

Tips:

- Customize your smoothie bowl with your favorite toppings for added flavor, texture, and nutrients.
- For a thicker smoothie base, use less liquid (water or juice) when blending.
- If you prefer a dairy-free or vegan smoothie bowl, use plant-based yogurt such as coconut or almond yogurt.
- Experiment with different combinations of melons and fruits to create unique flavor profiles.

This Melon Smoothie Bowl is not only delicious but also packed with vitamins, antioxidants, and hydration from the fresh melons. It's a perfect way to start your day or enjoy as a refreshing treat! Adjust the sweetness and toppings to suit your taste preferences.

Melon Fruit Salad

Ingredients:

- 1 small seedless watermelon, cubed
- 1 small cantaloupe melon, cubed
- 1 honeydew melon, cubed
- 1 cup strawberries, hulled and sliced
- 1 cup blueberries
- 1 cup grapes, halved
- Juice of 1 lime or lemon
- Fresh mint leaves, chopped (optional)
- Honey or agave syrup, to taste (optional)

Instructions:

Prepare the Melons and Fruits:
- Cut the seedless watermelon, cantaloupe, and honeydew melon into bite-sized cubes.
- Hull and slice the strawberries, wash the blueberries and grapes, and prepare them as needed.

Combine in a Bowl:
- In a large mixing bowl, combine all the cubed melons, strawberries, blueberries, and grapes.

Add Lime or Lemon Juice:
- Squeeze the juice of one lime or lemon over the fruit salad. The citrus juice will enhance the flavors and keep the fruits fresh.

Optional Sweetener:
- If desired, drizzle a little honey or agave syrup over the fruit salad to add sweetness. Adjust the amount based on the sweetness of the fruits.

Toss Gently:
- Gently toss the fruit salad to combine all the ingredients evenly.

Chill (Optional):
- Cover the bowl and refrigerate the fruit salad for about 30 minutes to allow the flavors to meld together.

Serve:
- Garnish the melon fruit salad with chopped fresh mint leaves, if desired.
- Serve chilled as a healthy and refreshing dessert or snack.

Tips:

- Feel free to customize the fruit salad with your favorite fruits such as pineapple, kiwi, mango, or raspberries.
- Add a sprinkle of toasted coconut flakes or chopped nuts for added texture.
- Make sure to use ripe and sweet melons for the best flavor.
- This fruit salad can be made ahead of time and stored in the refrigerator for a few hours before serving.

Enjoy this vibrant and delicious Melon Fruit Salad, perfect for summer picnics, BBQs, or any occasion where you want to serve a colorful and healthy dish! Adjust the ingredients and sweeteners based on your taste preferences.

Melon and Prosciutto Pizza

Ingredients:

For the Pizza Dough:

- 1 pound (16 oz) store-bought or homemade pizza dough

For the Toppings:

- 1/2 small seedless watermelon or cantaloupe, thinly sliced
- 6-8 slices of prosciutto, torn into pieces
- 8 ounces fresh mozzarella cheese, sliced or torn into pieces
- Handful of fresh basil leaves
- Balsamic glaze, for drizzling (optional)
- Olive oil, for brushing
- Salt and black pepper, to taste

Instructions:

Preheat the Oven:
- Preheat your oven to the temperature recommended for your pizza dough (usually around 450°F or as per dough instructions).

Prepare the Pizza Dough:
- Roll out the pizza dough on a lightly floured surface into your desired shape (round or rectangular) to fit your baking sheet or pizza stone.

Assemble the Pizza:
- Place the rolled-out dough onto a baking sheet or pizza stone.
- Brush the dough lightly with olive oil.

Add the Toppings:
- Arrange the thinly sliced melon over the pizza dough.
- Scatter torn pieces of prosciutto over the melon.
- Distribute the fresh mozzarella cheese evenly on top.
- Season with salt and black pepper to taste.

Bake the Pizza:
- Place the assembled pizza in the preheated oven.
- Bake for 12-15 minutes or until the crust is golden brown and the cheese is melted and bubbly.

Finish and Serve:

- Remove the pizza from the oven.
- Scatter fresh basil leaves over the hot pizza.
- Drizzle with balsamic glaze for added flavor and presentation (optional).

Slice and Enjoy:
- Allow the pizza to cool slightly before slicing.
- Serve warm and enjoy this delicious Melon and Prosciutto Pizza!

Tips:

- Feel free to use your favorite type of melon for this pizza, such as watermelon or cantaloupe.
- If you prefer a crispy crust, you can pre-bake the pizza dough for a few minutes before adding the toppings.
- Experiment with different cheeses like burrata or goat cheese for additional creaminess.
- Garnish with arugula or baby spinach for extra freshness and texture.

This Melon and Prosciutto Pizza is a perfect combination of sweet and savory flavors, ideal for a unique pizza night or special occasion. Enjoy the delicious contrast of melon and prosciutto with every bite!

Melon Granita

Ingredients:

- 1 medium-sized ripe melon (cantaloupe or honeydew)
- 1/2 cup granulated sugar (adjust to taste depending on the sweetness of the melon)
- 1/2 cup water
- Juice of 1 lemon (optional, for added brightness)

Instructions:

Prepare the Melon:
- Cut the melon in half, scoop out the seeds, and remove the rind. Cut the melon into chunks.

Make the Sugar Syrup:
- In a small saucepan, combine the sugar and water. Heat over medium heat, stirring until the sugar is completely dissolved. Remove from heat and let it cool.

Blend the Melon:
- Place the melon chunks in a blender or food processor. Add the cooled sugar syrup and lemon juice (if using). Blend until smooth.

Freezing the Granita:
- Pour the blended melon mixture into a shallow baking dish or a metal pan. The thinner the layer, the quicker it will freeze.
- Place the dish in the freezer. After about 45 minutes, check the mixture. When the edges start to freeze, scrape them with a fork and stir the mixture. Repeat this process every 30-45 minutes for about 3-4 hours, until the entire mixture is frozen and flaky.

Serve:
- Once the granita is fully frozen and has a fluffy texture, use a fork to scrape the entire mixture into light, icy crystals.
- Serve the melon granita in chilled glasses or bowls. Garnish with mint leaves or additional melon slices if desired.

Tips:

- You can experiment with different melon varieties for unique flavors.
- Adjust the sweetness by adding more or less sugar according to your taste and the sweetness of the melon.

- For a faster freezing process, use a metal baking dish and spread the mixture in a thin layer.
- Serve the granita immediately after scraping for the best texture.

Enjoy your homemade melon granita as a delightful and cooling dessert on a warm day!

Melon Granita

Ingredients:

- 1 ripe medium-sized melon (cantaloupe or honeydew)
- 1/2 cup granulated sugar (adjust based on sweetness of the melon)
- 1/2 cup water
- Juice of 1 lemon (optional, for added freshness)

Instructions:

Prepare the Melon:
- Cut the melon in half, scoop out the seeds, and remove the rind. Cut the melon flesh into chunks.

Make the Sugar Syrup:
- In a small saucepan, combine the granulated sugar and water. Heat over medium heat, stirring occasionally, until the sugar completely dissolves. Remove from heat and let it cool to room temperature.

Blend the Melon:
- Place the melon chunks into a blender or food processor. Add the cooled sugar syrup and lemon juice (if using). Blend until smooth.

Freezing the Granita:
- Pour the blended melon mixture into a shallow baking dish or a metal pan. The thinner the layer, the quicker it will freeze.

Freeze and Scrape:
- Place the dish in the freezer. After about 1 hour, check the mixture. When the edges start to freeze, use a fork to scrape and stir the mixture, breaking up any ice crystals.
- Continue to check and scrape the mixture every 30 minutes for about 2-3 hours, until the entire mixture is frozen and has a fluffy, granular texture.

Serve:
- Once the granita is fully frozen and flaky, use a fork to scrape the entire mixture into light, icy crystals.
- Serve the melon granita in chilled glasses or bowls. Garnish with fresh mint leaves or additional melon slices if desired.

Tips:

- For a quicker freezing process, use a metal baking dish and spread the mixture into a thin layer.

- Adjust the sweetness by adding more or less sugar depending on the natural sweetness of the melon.
- Feel free to experiment with different types of melon for unique flavors.
- Serve the granita immediately after scraping for the best texture.

Enjoy this homemade melon granita as a delightful and cooling treat on a sunny day!

Melon Ceviche

Ingredients:

- 1 ripe cantaloupe or honeydew melon
- 1/2 red onion, thinly sliced
- 1 cucumber, peeled and diced
- 1-2 jalapeño peppers, seeded and finely chopped (adjust based on spice preference)
- 1/4 cup fresh cilantro, chopped
- Juice of 2-3 limes
- Salt and pepper, to taste
- Optional additions: avocado chunks, cherry tomatoes, radishes

Instructions:

Prepare the Melon:
- Cut the melon in half, scoop out the seeds, and remove the rind. Cut the melon into small bite-sized cubes. Place the melon cubes in a large mixing bowl.

Add Vegetables and Herbs:
- Add the thinly sliced red onion, diced cucumber, chopped jalapeño peppers, and chopped cilantro to the bowl with the melon cubes.

Seasoning:
- Squeeze the juice of the limes over the melon and vegetable mixture. Start with the juice of 2 limes and add more if needed, based on your taste preference.
- Season with salt and pepper to taste. Mix everything gently to combine.

Marinate:
- Allow the melon ceviche to marinate in the refrigerator for at least 30 minutes to 1 hour. This allows the flavors to meld together and the melon to absorb the lime juice.

Serve:
- Once marinated, give the ceviche a final toss and taste for seasoning adjustments. Add more lime juice, salt, or pepper if desired.
- Serve the melon ceviche chilled in individual bowls or cups. Optionally, garnish with additional cilantro leaves.

Tips:

- You can customize this melon ceviche by adding other fresh ingredients like avocado chunks, halved cherry tomatoes, or thinly sliced radishes for extra crunch and flavor.
- Adjust the amount of jalapeño peppers based on your spice preference. If you prefer less heat, remove the seeds from the peppers before chopping.
- Serve the melon ceviche as a refreshing appetizer or light lunch. It pairs well with tortilla chips or crispy tostadas.
- Make sure to use ripe and sweet melon for the best flavor in this dish.

Enjoy this vibrant and unique melon ceviche for a delicious taste of summer!

Melon Mint Lemonade

Ingredients:

- 4 cups cubed ripe melon (cantaloupe, honeydew, or watermelon)
- 1/2 cup fresh lemon juice (from about 4-5 lemons)
- 1/2 cup granulated sugar (adjust to taste based on the sweetness of the melon)
- 4-5 cups cold water
- Fresh mint leaves, plus extra for garnish
- Ice cubes

Instructions:

Prepare the Melon:
- Cut the melon into cubes, removing the seeds and rind as needed.

Make the Melon Puree:
- In a blender, combine the cubed melon and fresh mint leaves. Blend until smooth and no large chunks remain.

Strain (Optional):
- If you prefer a smoother consistency, strain the melon puree through a fine mesh sieve or cheesecloth to remove any pulp. This step is optional, depending on your preference for texture.

Prepare the Lemonade Base:
- In a large pitcher, combine the fresh lemon juice and granulated sugar. Stir well until the sugar is dissolved.

Mix the Melon Puree:
- Pour the melon and mint puree into the pitcher with the lemon juice and sugar mixture. Stir to combine.

Add Cold Water:
- Gradually add the cold water to the pitcher, stirring continuously, until you reach your desired sweetness and concentration. Start with 4 cups of water and adjust based on taste.

Chill and Serve:
- Refrigerate the melon mint lemonade for at least 1 hour to chill and allow the flavors to meld.
- Before serving, taste the lemonade and adjust the sweetness or tartness by adding more sugar or lemon juice if needed.

Serve with Ice:
- Fill glasses with ice cubes and pour the chilled melon mint lemonade over the ice.

Garnish and Enjoy:
- Garnish each glass with a sprig of fresh mint leaves for added aroma and presentation.
- Stir the lemonade before serving to ensure the melon puree is evenly distributed.

Tips:

- Use ripe and sweet melons for the best flavor in this lemonade.
- Adjust the sweetness of the lemonade by varying the amount of sugar according to your taste preference and the sweetness of the melon.
- You can experiment with different types of melons or add a combination of melons for a unique flavor profile.
- For a sparkling version, replace some of the water with sparkling water or soda water.

Enjoy this cool and refreshing melon mint lemonade as a delightful summer drink!

Melon Sangria

Ingredients:

- 1 bottle (750 ml) of white wine (such as Sauvignon Blanc, Pinot Grigio, or Riesling)
- 2 cups cubed melon (cantaloupe, honeydew, or watermelon)
- 1/4 cup brandy or orange liqueur (e.g., Cointreau or Triple Sec)
- 1/4 cup simple syrup (made by dissolving equal parts sugar and water)
- Juice of 1-2 limes or lemons
- Fresh mint leaves, for garnish
- Sparkling water or club soda (optional, for a fizzy version)
- Ice cubes

Instructions:

Prepare the Melon:
- Wash and cube the melon of your choice into bite-sized pieces. Remove seeds and rind as needed.

Combine Ingredients:
- In a large pitcher, combine the cubed melon, white wine, brandy or orange liqueur, and simple syrup.
- Squeeze the juice of 1-2 limes or lemons into the pitcher. Adjust the amount of citrus juice based on your preference for tartness.

Stir and Chill:
- Stir the mixture well to combine all the ingredients. Cover the pitcher and refrigerate for at least 2-3 hours, or preferably overnight, to allow the flavors to meld together.

Serve:
- Before serving, taste the sangria and adjust the sweetness or tartness by adding more simple syrup or citrus juice if needed.
- If desired, add ice cubes to individual glasses to keep the sangria chilled while serving.

Optional Sparkling Version:
- For a fizzy melon sangria, top each glass with a splash of sparkling water or club soda just before serving.

Garnish and Enjoy:
- Garnish each glass with fresh mint leaves for a pop of color and aromatic freshness.

Tips:

- Use ripe and flavorful melons for the best results. You can use a combination of melons for a more complex flavor profile.
- Adjust the sweetness of the sangria according to your taste preference. If you prefer a sweeter sangria, add more simple syrup.
- Letting the sangria sit in the refrigerator overnight allows the flavors to develop and intensify.
- Feel free to add other fruits like berries or citrus slices to the sangria for additional flavor and visual appeal.

Enjoy this delicious and fruity melon sangria as a refreshing beverage for summer gatherings or outdoor parties! Adjust the recipe to suit your taste preferences and have fun experimenting with different types of melons and wine varieties.

Melon Bruschetta

Ingredients:

- 1 baguette, sliced into 1/2-inch thick rounds
- 2 cups cubed ripe melon (cantaloupe, honeydew, or watermelon)
- 1/2 cup crumbled feta cheese or goat cheese
- 1/4 cup fresh basil leaves, thinly sliced
- 2 tablespoons balsamic glaze or balsamic reduction
- 2 tablespoons extra virgin olive oil
- Salt and freshly ground black pepper, to taste

Instructions:

Prepare the Baguette Slices:
- Preheat the oven to 375°F (190°C). Arrange the baguette slices on a baking sheet and brush them lightly with olive oil. Bake in the preheated oven for 8-10 minutes, or until the slices are crisp and golden brown. Remove from the oven and set aside.

Prepare the Melon:
- Cut the melon into small, bite-sized cubes. Place the melon cubes in a mixing bowl.

Assemble the Bruschetta:
- In the bowl with the melon cubes, add the crumbled feta or goat cheese and thinly sliced basil leaves. Gently toss the ingredients together to combine.

Season and Dressing:
- Drizzle extra virgin olive oil over the melon mixture and season with salt and freshly ground black pepper, to taste. Toss again to evenly coat the ingredients.

Top the Baguette Slices:
- Arrange the toasted baguette slices on a serving platter or tray. Spoon the melon mixture generously onto each slice of baguette.

Finish with Balsamic Glaze:
- Drizzle balsamic glaze or balsamic reduction over the melon bruschetta. This adds a sweet and tangy flavor that complements the melon and cheese beautifully.

Garnish and Serve:
- Garnish the melon bruschetta with additional basil leaves for a pop of color and freshness.

Tips:

- Choose ripe and flavorful melons for the best taste in this bruschetta.
- Feel free to experiment with different types of cheeses such as ricotta, mozzarella, or Parmesan if you prefer a different flavor profile.
- You can add a touch of honey or a sprinkle of red pepper flakes for a variation in flavor.
- Serve the melon bruschetta immediately to enjoy the contrast of textures and flavors while the baguette slices are still crisp.

This melon bruschetta makes a delightful appetizer for parties or gatherings, offering a perfect balance of sweet melon, creamy cheese, and aromatic basil on crispy baguette slices. Enjoy this elegant and flavorful dish!

Melon Popsicles

Ingredients:

- 4 cups cubed ripe melon (cantaloupe, honeydew, or watermelon)
- 1/4 cup honey or agave syrup (adjust based on sweetness of the melon)
- Juice of 1 lime or lemon
- Optional: Fresh mint leaves or basil leaves for added flavor

Instructions:

Prepare the Melon:
- Wash and cut the melon into small cubes, removing the seeds and rind as needed.

Blend the Melon Mixture:
- In a blender or food processor, combine the cubed melon, honey or agave syrup, and lime or lemon juice.
- Optionally, add a few fresh mint leaves or basil leaves for added freshness and flavor.

Blend Until Smooth:
- Blend the ingredients until you achieve a smooth and well-combined mixture.

Fill Popsicle Molds:
- Pour the melon mixture into popsicle molds, leaving a little space at the top for expansion.

Insert Popsicle Sticks:
- Place popsicle sticks into each mold, ensuring they are centered and can stand upright.

Freeze Until Solid:
- Place the filled popsicle molds in the freezer and let them freeze completely for at least 4-6 hours, or preferably overnight.

Unmold and Serve:
- Once the melon popsicles are fully frozen and solid, remove them from the molds.
- To release the popsicles, run the molds briefly under warm water or dip them in warm water to loosen the popsicles.

Enjoy:
- Serve the melon popsicles immediately and enjoy these refreshing treats on a hot day!

Tips:

- Choose ripe and sweet melons for the best flavor in your popsicles.
- Adjust the sweetness by varying the amount of honey or agave syrup based on the natural sweetness of the melon.
- Feel free to experiment with different types of melons or add other fruits like berries or citrus for a flavor variation.
- For added visual appeal, consider adding small fruit pieces into the popsicle molds before pouring in the melon mixture.

These homemade melon popsicles are perfect for cooling down and enjoying a healthy, fruity treat. They are easy to make and can be customized to suit your taste preferences. Enjoy!

Melon and Shrimp Salad

Ingredients:

- 1 pound large shrimp, peeled and deveined
- 4 cups cubed ripe melon (cantaloupe, honeydew, or watermelon)
- 1/2 English cucumber, thinly sliced
- 1/4 red onion, thinly sliced
- 1/4 cup fresh mint leaves, chopped
- 1/4 cup fresh cilantro leaves, chopped
- Juice of 2 limes
- 2 tablespoons extra virgin olive oil
- Salt and pepper, to taste
- Optional: Red chili flakes or hot sauce for added spice

Instructions:

Cook the Shrimp:
- Bring a pot of salted water to a boil. Add the shrimp and cook for 2-3 minutes, or until pink and opaque. Drain the shrimp and rinse under cold water to stop the cooking process. Pat dry with paper towels.

Prepare the Salad Ingredients:
- In a large mixing bowl, combine the cubed melon, sliced cucumber, sliced red onion, chopped mint leaves, and chopped cilantro leaves.

Make the Dressing:
- In a small bowl, whisk together the lime juice, extra virgin olive oil, salt, and pepper. Adjust the seasoning to taste. If you like it spicy, add red chili flakes or hot sauce.

Assemble the Salad:
- Add the cooked and cooled shrimp to the bowl with the melon mixture.

Toss with Dressing:
- Pour the dressing over the salad ingredients. Gently toss everything together until well combined and evenly coated with the dressing.

Chill and Serve:
- Cover the salad and refrigerate for at least 30 minutes to allow the flavors to meld together and the salad to chill.

Serve:
- Serve the melon and shrimp salad in individual bowls or on a platter.
- Garnish with additional fresh herbs and lime wedges if desired.

Tips:

- Use ripe and sweet melons for the best flavor in this salad.
- Feel free to substitute the herbs with other favorites like basil or parsley.
- Adjust the amount of lime juice and olive oil in the dressing to suit your taste preferences.
- This salad can be served as a light lunch or dinner, or as a refreshing appetizer for parties and gatherings.

Enjoy this flavorful and refreshing melon and shrimp salad as a delicious and healthy meal option! The combination of sweet melon, succulent shrimp, and fresh herbs is sure to be a hit.

Melon Stuffed with Chicken Salad

Ingredients:

- 1 whole cantaloupe or honeydew melon
- 2 cups cooked chicken breast, diced or shredded
- 1/2 cup mayonnaise
- 1 celery stalk, finely chopped
- 1/4 cup red onion, finely chopped
- 1/4 cup dried cranberries or grapes, halved
- 1/4 cup chopped pecans or walnuts (optional)
- Salt and pepper, to taste
- Fresh lettuce leaves, for serving
- Fresh parsley or mint leaves, for garnish

Instructions:

Prepare the Melon:
- Cut the cantaloupe or honeydew melon in half and scoop out the seeds. Use a melon baller or spoon to scoop out some of the flesh from each half, creating a hollow cavity for the chicken salad. Reserve the melon balls for garnish or snacking.

Make the Chicken Salad:
- In a mixing bowl, combine the diced or shredded cooked chicken breast, chopped celery, chopped red onion, dried cranberries or halved grapes, and chopped nuts (if using).
- Add mayonnaise to the mixture and stir until everything is well coated and combined. Adjust the amount of mayonnaise based on your preference for creaminess.

Season the Salad:
- Season the chicken salad with salt and pepper to taste. Stir well to incorporate the seasoning.

Fill the Melon Halves:
- Divide the chicken salad mixture evenly between the hollowed-out melon halves, mounding the salad in the center.

Chill the Stuffed Melon:
- Cover the stuffed melon halves with plastic wrap and refrigerate for at least 1 hour to chill and allow the flavors to meld together.

Serve:

- To serve, line serving plates with fresh lettuce leaves. Carefully place each stuffed melon half on top of the lettuce.

Garnish and Enjoy:
- Garnish the stuffed melon halves with reserved melon balls, fresh parsley or mint leaves, and additional dried cranberries or nuts if desired.

Tips:

- Choose a ripe and sweet melon for the best flavor and texture in this dish.
- Feel free to customize the chicken salad by adding other ingredients such as chopped apples, sliced grapes, or diced bell peppers.
- Serve this dish as an elegant and refreshing appetizer or light lunch option.
- For a variation, you can use other types of protein such as tuna or shrimp instead of chicken.

This melon stuffed with chicken salad is a delightful and creative way to enjoy a summer meal. The combination of sweet melon and savory chicken salad creates a perfect balance of flavors and textures. Enjoy this dish with family and friends!

Melon Margarita

Ingredients:

- 2 oz silver tequila
- 1 oz triple sec or orange liqueur
- 1 cup cubed ripe melon (cantaloupe, honeydew, or watermelon)
- Juice of 1 lime
- 1-2 teaspoons agave syrup or simple syrup (adjust to taste)
- Ice
- Salt or Tajín (chili-lime seasoning) for rimming the glass (optional)
- Lime wedges or melon balls for garnish (optional)

Instructions:

Prepare the Melon:
- Cut the melon into small cubes. Reserve a few pieces for garnish if desired.

Blend the Margarita:
- In a blender, combine the cubed melon, tequila, triple sec (or orange liqueur), lime juice, and agave syrup (or simple syrup).
- Add ice to the blender, enough to fill about halfway.

Blend Until Smooth:
- Blend the ingredients until smooth and well combined. Taste and adjust sweetness by adding more agave syrup if needed.

Prepare the Glass:
- Optional: Rim a glass with salt or Tajín by rubbing the rim with a lime wedge and dipping it into the seasoning.

Pour and Serve:
- Fill the prepared glass with ice.
- Pour the blended melon margarita mixture into the glass.

Garnish:
- Garnish the margarita with a lime wedge or melon balls on the rim of the glass.

Serve and Enjoy:
- Serve the Melon Margarita immediately and enjoy this refreshing cocktail!

Tips:

- Use ripe and flavorful melon for the best taste in this margarita.

- Adjust the sweetness and tartness by varying the amount of lime juice and agave syrup according to your taste preference.
- For a spicy twist, add a slice of jalapeño or a dash of chili powder to the blender.
- If you prefer a frozen margarita, use more ice and blend until slushy consistency.

This Melon Margarita is perfect for enjoying during warm weather or as a fun cocktail for parties and gatherings. It's a delightful blend of sweet melon and zesty lime flavors with a kick of tequila. Cheers!

Melon and Avocado Salad

Ingredients:

- 4 cups cubed ripe melon (cantaloupe, honeydew, or watermelon)
- 2 ripe avocados, peeled, pitted, and diced
- 1/4 cup red onion, thinly sliced
- 1/4 cup fresh mint leaves, chopped
- 1/4 cup crumbled feta cheese (optional)
- Juice of 1 lime
- 2 tablespoons extra virgin olive oil
- Salt and pepper, to taste
- Optional: Toasted pepitas (pumpkin seeds) or chopped nuts for added crunch

Instructions:

Prepare the Salad Ingredients:
- In a large mixing bowl, combine the cubed melon, diced avocados, thinly sliced red onion, and chopped fresh mint leaves.

Make the Dressing:
- In a small bowl, whisk together the lime juice, extra virgin olive oil, salt, and pepper until well combined.

Assemble the Salad:
- Drizzle the dressing over the salad ingredients in the bowl.
- Gently toss the salad to coat everything evenly with the dressing.

Add Optional Ingredients:
- If using crumbled feta cheese, sprinkle it over the salad and toss gently.
- Optionally, sprinkle toasted pepitas or chopped nuts over the salad for added texture and flavor.

Serve and Enjoy:
- Transfer the salad to a serving platter or bowl.
- Garnish with additional fresh mint leaves.
- Serve the melon and avocado salad immediately and enjoy!

Tips:

- Choose ripe and flavorful melons and avocados for the best taste and texture in this salad.
- Adjust the dressing ingredients (lime juice, olive oil, salt, and pepper) based on your taste preferences.

- The feta cheese adds a nice salty flavor to the salad, but you can omit it or substitute with goat cheese or queso fresco if desired.
- Feel free to customize this salad by adding other ingredients such as cherry tomatoes, cucumber slices, or arugula.
- Serve this salad as a side dish with grilled chicken or fish, or enjoy it as a light and healthy lunch option.

This melon and avocado salad is a delightful combination of flavors and textures, perfect for summer gatherings or anytime you want a refreshing and nutritious dish. Enjoy!

Melon Panzanella

Ingredients:

- 1 small loaf of crusty bread (like ciabatta or sourdough), cut into cubes (about 4 cups)
- 4 cups cubed ripe melon (cantaloupe, honeydew, or watermelon)
- 1/2 red onion, thinly sliced
- 1 cucumber, sliced into half-moons
- 1/2 cup fresh basil leaves, torn or chopped
- 1/4 cup chopped fresh mint leaves
- 1/4 cup crumbled feta cheese (optional)
- 1/4 cup extra virgin olive oil
- 3 tablespoons red wine vinegar or balsamic vinegar
- Salt and pepper, to taste

Instructions:

Prepare the Bread Cubes:
- Preheat the oven to 375°F (190°C). Place the bread cubes on a baking sheet and drizzle with 2 tablespoons of olive oil. Toss to coat evenly. Bake in the preheated oven for 10-15 minutes, or until the bread cubes are golden and crispy. Remove from the oven and let them cool.

Assemble the Salad:
- In a large mixing bowl, combine the cubed melon, sliced red onion, cucumber slices, torn basil leaves, chopped mint leaves, and crumbled feta cheese (if using).

Make the Dressing:
- In a small bowl, whisk together the remaining 2 tablespoons of olive oil with the red wine vinegar or balsamic vinegar. Season with salt and pepper to taste.

Combine Everything:
- Add the cooled bread cubes to the bowl with the melon and vegetables.
- Pour the dressing over the salad ingredients.

Toss and Let Sit:
- Gently toss all the ingredients together until well combined and the bread cubes are coated with the dressing.
- Let the panzanella sit for about 10-15 minutes to allow the flavors to meld together.

Serve and Enjoy:

- Divide the melon panzanella into individual serving bowls or plates.
- Garnish with additional fresh basil leaves or mint leaves if desired.
- Serve immediately and enjoy this delicious and refreshing salad!

Tips:

- Use ripe and flavorful melon for the best taste and sweetness in this salad.
- You can customize this salad by adding other ingredients such as cherry tomatoes, bell peppers, or olives.
- If you prefer a vegan version, omit the feta cheese or substitute with vegan cheese or toasted nuts/seeds.
- Melon panzanella is best enjoyed fresh but can be stored in the refrigerator for a few hours before serving. The bread may soften slightly over time.

This melon panzanella is a wonderful way to celebrate the flavors of summer. It's perfect for picnics, barbecues, or as a light and refreshing side dish for any meal. Enjoy!

Melon Tuna Poke Bowl

Ingredients:

For the Poke:

- 1 pound sushi-grade tuna, cut into bite-sized cubes
- 1/4 cup soy sauce
- 1 tablespoon sesame oil
- 1 tablespoon rice vinegar
- 1 teaspoon grated fresh ginger
- 2 green onions, thinly sliced
- 1/2 teaspoon red pepper flakes (optional, for spice)
- 2 cups cubed ripe melon (cantaloupe, honeydew, or watermelon)
- Cooked sushi rice or brown rice, for serving

For the Garnish:

- Sliced avocado
- Sliced cucumber
- Shredded nori (seaweed)
- Toasted sesame seeds
- Pickled ginger
- Wasabi (optional)

Instructions:

Prepare the Tuna Poke:
- In a mixing bowl, combine the soy sauce, sesame oil, rice vinegar, grated ginger, sliced green onions, and red pepper flakes (if using).
- Add the tuna cubes to the bowl and gently toss to coat the tuna in the marinade. Cover and refrigerate for at least 30 minutes to marinate.

Assemble the Poke Bowl:
- Cook sushi rice or brown rice according to package instructions. Divide the cooked rice among serving bowls.

Add Melon and Tuna:

- Remove the marinated tuna from the refrigerator. Add the cubed melon to the bowl with the tuna and gently toss to combine.

Assemble the Bowl:
- Arrange the marinated tuna and melon mixture over the rice in each bowl.
- Top the bowls with sliced avocado, sliced cucumber, shredded nori, and toasted sesame seeds.

Garnish and Serve:
- Garnish each bowl with pickled ginger and a small dollop of wasabi (if desired).
- Serve the Melon Tuna Poke Bowls immediately and enjoy!

Tips:

- Use sushi-grade tuna for the best flavor and texture in this dish.
- Feel free to customize the toppings based on your preference. You can add edamame, radishes, mango slices, or other fresh ingredients.
- Adjust the level of spiciness by adding more or less red pepper flakes or including a drizzle of sriracha sauce.
- This dish is best enjoyed fresh but can be prepared ahead of time and stored in the refrigerator until ready to serve.

This Melon Tuna Poke Bowl is a delightful and nutritious meal option, combining the flavors of fresh tuna, sweet melon, and a variety of colorful toppings. It's perfect for lunch or dinner and sure to impress! Adjust the ingredients to suit your taste preferences and enjoy this tasty poke bowl creation.

Melon and Cucumber Gazpacho

Ingredients:

- 4 cups cubed ripe melon (cantaloupe, honeydew, or watermelon)
- 2 medium cucumbers, peeled and diced
- 1/2 small red onion, diced
- 1 red bell pepper, seeded and diced
- 2 cloves garlic, minced
- 2 tablespoons fresh lime juice
- 2 tablespoons white wine vinegar
- 1/4 cup extra virgin olive oil
- Salt and pepper, to taste
- Fresh mint leaves or basil leaves, for garnish
- Optional toppings: diced avocado, crumbled feta cheese, or toasted bread cubes

Instructions:

Prepare the Ingredients:
- In a blender or food processor, combine the cubed melon, diced cucumbers, red onion, red bell pepper, and minced garlic.

Blend the Soup:
- Blend the ingredients until smooth and well combined. You may need to work in batches depending on the size of your blender.

Add Lime Juice and Vinegar:
- Add the fresh lime juice and white wine vinegar to the blended mixture. Blend again to incorporate.

Season and Chill:
- While blending, drizzle in the extra virgin olive oil to emulsify the soup. Season with salt and pepper to taste.
- Transfer the gazpacho to a large bowl or container. Cover and refrigerate for at least 1 hour to chill and allow the flavors to meld together.

Serve:
- Stir the gazpacho before serving to ensure it's well mixed.
- Ladle the chilled gazpacho into bowls or glasses.
- Garnish with fresh mint leaves or basil leaves.

Add Optional Toppings:
- If desired, top the gazpacho with diced avocado, crumbled feta cheese, or toasted bread cubes for added texture and flavor.

Enjoy:

- Serve the melon and cucumber gazpacho cold and enjoy this refreshing summer soup!

Tips:

- Use ripe and flavorful melon and cucumbers for the best taste in this gazpacho.
- Adjust the amount of lime juice and vinegar based on your preference for acidity.
- Feel free to customize this gazpacho by adding other ingredients such as jalapeño peppers for heat or fresh herbs like cilantro or parsley.
- This soup can be made ahead of time and stored in the refrigerator for up to 2 days. Stir well before serving.

This melon and cucumber gazpacho is a light and healthy dish that's bursting with flavor. It's perfect as a starter for a summer meal or as a refreshing snack. Enjoy this chilled soup on a warm day!

Melon and Mint Infused Water

Ingredients:

- 2 cups cubed ripe melon (cantaloupe, honeydew, or watermelon)
- Fresh mint leaves, washed
- 4 cups water (filtered or spring water recommended)
- Ice cubes (optional)

Instructions:

Prepare the Ingredients:
- Wash and cut the melon into small cubes. Remove seeds and rind as needed.
- Wash the fresh mint leaves and pat them dry.

Combine Melon and Mint:
- In a pitcher or large jar, add the cubed melon and fresh mint leaves.

Muddle the Ingredients:
- Use a muddler or the back of a spoon to gently press on the melon and mint leaves. This helps release their flavors into the water.

Add Water:
- Pour the water into the pitcher or jar, covering the melon and mint.

Refrigerate to Infuse:
- Cover the pitcher or jar and place it in the refrigerator.
- Let the water infuse for at least 1-2 hours, or ideally overnight for stronger flavor.

Serve and Enjoy:
- When ready to serve, give the infused water a gentle stir.
- Pour the infused water into glasses filled with ice cubes (if desired).

Garnish (Optional):
- Garnish each glass with a sprig of fresh mint or a slice of melon for a decorative touch.

Variations:
- For added flavor, you can also try adding a few slices of cucumber or a squeeze of fresh lime juice to the infused water.

Tips:

- Choose ripe and sweet melon for the best flavor in this infused water.
- Adjust the amount of mint leaves based on your preference for minty flavor.

- Infused water can be kept refrigerated for up to 2 days. The longer it sits, the stronger the flavors will become.
- This melon and mint infused water is a great alternative to sugary beverages and is perfect for staying hydrated throughout the day.

Enjoy this refreshing and naturally flavored melon and mint infused water as a healthy and delicious drink option! It's a wonderful way to stay cool and hydrated, especially during warm weather.

Melon Jelly

Ingredients:

- 4 cups of melon juice (from pureed and strained melon)
- 1/4 cup freshly squeezed lemon juice
- 1 package (1.75 oz) powdered fruit pectin
- 5 cups granulated sugar
- Optional: Food coloring (if desired for a more vibrant color)

Instructions:

Prepare the Melon Juice:
- Wash and cut ripe melons (cantaloupe, honeydew, or watermelon) into chunks. Puree the melon chunks in a blender or food processor until smooth.
- Strain the pureed melon through a fine mesh sieve or cheesecloth to extract the juice. You'll need 4 cups of melon juice for this recipe.

Prepare the Canning Equipment:
- Sterilize canning jars and lids by boiling them in a large pot of water for at least 10 minutes. Keep them hot until ready to use.

Cook the Jelly Mixture:
- In a large pot, combine the melon juice, lemon juice, and powdered fruit pectin. Stir well to dissolve the pectin.
- Place the pot over medium-high heat and bring the mixture to a rolling boil, stirring constantly.

Add Sugar:
- Gradually add the granulated sugar to the boiling mixture, stirring continuously. Stir until the sugar is completely dissolved.

Boil and Test for Doneness:
- Continue boiling the mixture for 1-2 minutes, stirring constantly. To test for doneness, place a small amount of the jelly mixture on a chilled plate and tilt the plate. If the jelly wrinkles and holds its shape, it's ready.

Remove from Heat and Skim Foam:
- Remove the pot from the heat and skim off any foam that has formed on the surface of the jelly.

Fill and Seal Jars:
- Carefully ladle the hot melon jelly into the sterilized canning jars, leaving about 1/4-inch headspace at the top.

- Wipe the jar rims clean with a damp cloth to ensure a proper seal. Place the lids on the jars and tighten the bands.

Process the Jars (Optional):
- If you'd like to store the jelly long-term at room temperature, process the jars in a boiling water bath for 10 minutes. Ensure the jars are completely submerged in water during processing.

Cool and Store:
- Allow the jars to cool completely at room temperature. Check that the lids have sealed properly (they should not flex when pressed in the center). Store the sealed jars in a cool, dark place.

Enjoy Your Melon Jelly:
- Once cooled and set, your melon jelly is ready to enjoy! Serve it on toast, biscuits, or use it in desserts and recipes.

Tips:

- Use ripe and flavorful melons for the best-tasting jelly.
- Feel free to experiment with different types of melons or add spices like cinnamon or ginger for additional flavor.
- Properly sealed jars of melon jelly can be stored in a cool, dark place for up to a year. Once opened, store in the refrigerator and use within a few weeks.

Enjoy your homemade melon jelly spread on breakfast treats or as a delightful addition to your culinary creations!

Melon Yogurt Parfait

Ingredients:

- 2 cups cubed ripe melon (cantaloupe, honeydew, or watermelon)
- 2 cups plain Greek yogurt
- 1 cup granola (store-bought or homemade)
- Honey or agave syrup, to taste (optional)
- Fresh mint leaves, for garnish (optional)

Instructions:

Prepare the Melon:
- Wash and cut the melon into small, bite-sized cubes. You can use cantaloupe, honeydew, or watermelon for this recipe. Ensure the melon is ripe and sweet.

Assemble the Parfaits:
- In serving glasses or bowls, start layering the ingredients.
- Begin with a layer of cubed melon at the bottom of each glass.

Add Yogurt Layer:
- Spoon a layer of plain Greek yogurt over the melon cubes. You can sweeten the yogurt with a drizzle of honey or agave syrup if desired.

Add Granola Layer:
- Sprinkle a layer of granola over the yogurt. The granola adds a nice crunch and texture to the parfait.

Repeat Layers:
- Continue layering with another layer of melon cubes, followed by yogurt, and then granola.

Finish with Toppings:
- Top each parfait with a final layer of melon cubes.
- Garnish with fresh mint leaves for a pop of color and added freshness.

Serve and Enjoy:
- Serve the melon yogurt parfaits immediately and enjoy this refreshing and nutritious treat!

Tips:

- Customize your parfaits by using different types of melons or adding other fruits like berries or sliced bananas.

- Experiment with flavored yogurts such as vanilla or honey-flavored Greek yogurt for added sweetness.
- If you prefer a dairy-free option, use coconut yogurt or almond milk yogurt instead of Greek yogurt.
- Feel free to add additional toppings such as sliced almonds, coconut flakes, or a sprinkle of cinnamon for extra flavor.

These melon yogurt parfaits are perfect for breakfast, a healthy snack, or a light dessert. They're easy to assemble and can be prepared ahead of time for a quick and satisfying treat. Enjoy the combination of sweet melon, creamy yogurt, and crunchy granola in every spoonful!

Melon and Goat Cheese Crostini

Ingredients:

- 1 French baguette, sliced into 1/2-inch thick rounds
- Olive oil, for brushing
- 4 ounces soft goat cheese
- 2 cups cubed ripe melon (cantaloupe, honeydew, or watermelon)
- Fresh basil leaves, thinly sliced
- Balsamic glaze, for drizzling (optional)
- Salt and black pepper, to taste

Instructions:

Prepare the Baguette Slices:
- Preheat the oven to 375°F (190°C).
- Place the baguette slices on a baking sheet in a single layer.
- Brush both sides of the baguette slices with olive oil.
- Bake in the preheated oven for about 8-10 minutes, or until the slices are golden and crispy. Remove from the oven and let them cool slightly.

Assemble the Crostini:
- Spread a generous amount of soft goat cheese onto each toasted baguette slice.

Add Melon Cubes:
- Arrange the cubed melon on top of the goat cheese layer on each crostini.

Season and Garnish:
- Sprinkle a little salt and black pepper over the melon cubes.
- Top each crostini with thinly sliced fresh basil leaves.

Drizzle with Balsamic Glaze (Optional):
- For added flavor, drizzle a small amount of balsamic glaze over the assembled crostini.

Serve and Enjoy:
- Arrange the melon and goat cheese crostini on a serving platter.
- Serve immediately and enjoy this delicious appetizer!

Tips:

- Use ripe and flavorful melon for the best taste in this appetizer.
- Feel free to substitute the goat cheese with cream cheese or ricotta if preferred.

- Customize the crostini by adding additional toppings such as prosciutto slices or a sprinkle of crushed red pepper flakes for a touch of heat.
- If you don't have balsamic glaze, you can use a balsamic reduction or simply omit this step.

These melon and goat cheese crostini are a wonderful combination of sweet, creamy, and savory flavors. They make a beautiful and tasty addition to any party or gathering.

Enjoy this elegant appetizer with family and friends!

Melon Chutney

Ingredients:

- 4 cups cubed ripe melon (cantaloupe, honeydew, or watermelon)
- 1 medium onion, finely chopped
- 1/2 cup raisins or dried cranberries
- 1/2 cup apple cider vinegar
- 1 cup brown sugar
- 1 tablespoon fresh ginger, grated
- 1 teaspoon mustard seeds
- 1/2 teaspoon ground cinnamon
- 1/4 teaspoon ground cloves
- 1/4 teaspoon salt
- Pinch of cayenne pepper (optional, for heat)

Instructions:

Prepare the Ingredients:
- Wash and cut the melon into small cubes. Finely chop the onion and grate the fresh ginger.

Cook the Chutney:
- In a large saucepan or pot, combine the cubed melon, chopped onion, raisins or dried cranberries, apple cider vinegar, brown sugar, grated ginger, mustard seeds, ground cinnamon, ground cloves, salt, and cayenne pepper (if using).

Simmer the Mixture:
- Place the saucepan over medium heat and bring the mixture to a simmer, stirring occasionally.

Reduce and Cook:
- Reduce the heat to low and let the chutney simmer gently for about 45-60 minutes, or until the mixture thickens and the flavors meld together. Stir occasionally to prevent sticking.

Check the Consistency:
- The chutney is ready when it has a thick, jam-like consistency. If it's too runny, continue to simmer until desired thickness is achieved.

Cool and Store:
- Remove the pot from the heat and let the chutney cool completely.
- Transfer the cooled chutney into clean, sterilized jars or containers.

Serve or Store:

- Refrigerate the melon chutney for up to several weeks. This allows the flavors to further develop.
- Serve the melon chutney as a condiment with grilled meats, sandwiches, cheese platters, or as a topping for crackers or toast.

Tips:

- Use ripe and sweet melon for the best flavor in this chutney.
- Adjust the sweetness and tanginess by varying the amount of brown sugar and apple cider vinegar.
- Feel free to customize the chutney by adding other ingredients such as chopped apples, chopped dried apricots, or a splash of orange juice.
- This melon chutney makes a wonderful homemade gift when packaged in decorative jars with a ribbon.

Enjoy this delicious and versatile melon chutney as a flavorful addition to your meals and snacks! Its sweet and savory flavors will complement a wide range of dishes and elevate your culinary creations.

Melon Mousse

Ingredients:

- 2 cups cubed ripe melon (cantaloupe, honeydew, or watermelon)
- 1 tablespoon lemon juice
- 1 envelope (about 2 1/4 teaspoons) unflavored gelatin
- 1/4 cup cold water
- 1/2 cup granulated sugar
- 1 cup heavy cream
- Mint leaves, for garnish (optional)

Instructions:

Prepare the Melon Puree:
- In a blender or food processor, puree the cubed melon until smooth. Add the lemon juice to the melon puree and blend again to combine.

Bloom the Gelatin:
- In a small bowl, sprinkle the gelatin over the cold water. Let it sit for about 5 minutes to bloom and soften.

Heat the Gelatin Mixture:
- After the gelatin has bloomed, transfer the bowl to a microwave or place it in a small saucepan over low heat. Warm the gelatin mixture just until the gelatin is dissolved, stirring constantly. Be careful not to boil the mixture.

Combine the Melon Puree and Gelatin:
- In a large mixing bowl, whisk together the melon puree and dissolved gelatin mixture until well combined.

Whip the Heavy Cream:
- In a separate bowl, using an electric mixer or whisk, whip the heavy cream until soft peaks form. Gradually add the granulated sugar while continuing to whip until stiff peaks form.

Fold in the Whipped Cream:
- Gently fold the whipped cream into the melon mixture using a spatula or whisk. Be gentle to maintain the airy texture of the mousse.

Chill the Mousse:
- Transfer the melon mousse mixture into serving glasses or bowls. Cover with plastic wrap and refrigerate for at least 2-3 hours, or until the mousse is set.

Serve and Garnish:
- Remove the chilled melon mousse from the refrigerator.

- Garnish with fresh mint leaves or additional melon cubes if desired.
- Serve chilled and enjoy this light and delicious melon mousse!

Tips:

- Choose ripe and flavorful melons for the best taste in this mousse.
- Feel free to experiment with different varieties of melons to create unique flavor combinations.
- For a dairy-free version, substitute the heavy cream with coconut cream or a dairy-free whipped topping.
- You can adjust the sweetness of the mousse by varying the amount of sugar according to your taste preference.

This melon mousse is a delightful dessert that's perfect for summer gatherings or special occasions. Its smooth and airy texture combined with the natural sweetness of melons makes it a crowd-pleaser. Enjoy this refreshing treat!

Melon and Basil Salad

Ingredients:

- 4 cups cubed ripe melon (cantaloupe, honeydew, or watermelon)
- 1/2 cup fresh basil leaves, thinly sliced or torn
- 1/4 cup crumbled feta cheese (optional)
- 2 tablespoons extra virgin olive oil
- 1 tablespoon balsamic vinegar
- Salt and black pepper, to taste
- Optional: Toasted pine nuts or chopped walnuts for added crunch

Instructions:

Prepare the Melon and Basil:
- Wash, peel (if necessary), and cube the ripe melon into bite-sized pieces.
- Wash the fresh basil leaves and thinly slice or tear them into smaller pieces.

Assemble the Salad:
- In a large salad bowl, combine the cubed melon and sliced basil leaves.
- If using, add the crumbled feta cheese to the bowl.

Make the Dressing:
- In a small bowl, whisk together the extra virgin olive oil and balsamic vinegar to create the dressing.
- Season the dressing with salt and black pepper, to taste.

Combine and Toss:
- Drizzle the dressing over the melon and basil mixture.
- Gently toss the salad ingredients together until everything is well coated with the dressing.

Add Optional Toppings:
- If desired, sprinkle toasted pine nuts or chopped walnuts over the salad for added crunch and flavor.

Serve and Enjoy:
- Transfer the melon and basil salad to serving plates or bowls.
- Serve immediately and enjoy this light and refreshing summer salad!

Tips:

- Choose ripe and flavorful melons for the best taste in this salad.

- Feel free to customize the salad by adding other ingredients such as cucumber slices, cherry tomatoes, or red onion for additional flavor and texture.
- If you prefer a sweeter flavor profile, you can drizzle a touch of honey or maple syrup over the salad dressing.
- This salad pairs well with grilled chicken, fish, or as a side dish for picnics and barbecues.

This melon and basil salad is a delightful combination of flavors and textures. It's quick and easy to prepare, making it a perfect dish for any occasion. Enjoy this refreshing salad as a light and healthy addition to your summer meals!

Melon Brulee

Ingredients:

- 1 ripe cantaloupe melon
- Granulated sugar, for caramelizing
- Fresh mint leaves, for garnish (optional)

Instructions:

    Prepare the Melon:
- Slice the cantaloupe melon in half and remove the seeds.
- Use a melon baller to scoop out small balls of melon flesh. Alternatively, you can cut the melon into small cubes.

    Arrange the Melon:
- Divide the melon balls or cubes into individual serving dishes or ramekins, filling them up to about 3/4 full.

    Caramelize the Sugar:
- Sprinkle a thin, even layer of granulated sugar over the top of each serving of melon.
- Use a kitchen torch to carefully caramelize the sugar. Hold the torch about 2-3 inches away from the sugar and move it in a circular motion until the sugar melts and caramelizes. Be cautious not to burn the sugar or overheat the melon.

    Chill and Set:
- Place the caramelized melon brûlée dishes in the refrigerator for about 10-15 minutes to allow the sugar to harden and create a crispy caramelized crust.

    Garnish and Serve:
- Once chilled, garnish the melon brûlée with fresh mint leaves for a pop of color and added freshness.
- Serve immediately and enjoy this unique and delightful dessert!

Tips:

- Choose a ripe and sweet cantaloupe melon for the best flavor and texture in this dessert.
- You can use a kitchen torch to caramelize the sugar, or if you don't have a torch, you can place the melon dishes under the broiler for a few seconds until the sugar caramelizes.

- Experiment with different types of melons such as honeydew or watermelon for variations of this dessert.
- Serve the melon brûlée as a light and refreshing dessert on its own or with a dollop of whipped cream or a scoop of vanilla ice cream for added indulgence.

Enjoy this elegant and delicious melon brûlée as a creative and refreshing dessert that's perfect for summer gatherings or special occasions!

Melon Teriyaki Chicken Skewers

Ingredients:

- 1 pound boneless, skinless chicken breasts, cut into bite-sized pieces
- 2 cups cubed ripe melon (cantaloupe, honeydew, or watermelon)
- Wooden skewers, soaked in water for 30 minutes (or use metal skewers)

For the Teriyaki Marinade:

- 1/2 cup soy sauce
- 1/4 cup honey or brown sugar
- 2 tablespoons rice vinegar
- 2 cloves garlic, minced
- 1 tablespoon grated fresh ginger
- 1 tablespoon sesame oil
- 2 tablespoons water
- 1 tablespoon cornstarch
- Sesame seeds, for garnish (optional)
- Sliced green onions, for garnish (optional)

Instructions:

Prepare the Teriyaki Marinade:
- In a small saucepan, combine soy sauce, honey or brown sugar, rice vinegar, minced garlic, grated ginger, and sesame oil.
- In a separate bowl, mix water and cornstarch until well combined to create a slurry.
- Heat the saucepan over medium heat and bring the mixture to a simmer.
- Slowly whisk in the cornstarch slurry, stirring constantly, until the sauce thickens. Remove from heat and set aside.

Marinate the Chicken:
- Place the chicken pieces in a bowl or resealable plastic bag.
- Pour half of the teriyaki marinade over the chicken, reserving the other half for later use.
- Toss the chicken to coat evenly in the marinade. Cover and refrigerate for at least 30 minutes (or up to 2 hours) to marinate.

Assemble the Skewers:
- Preheat the grill or broiler.

- Thread the marinated chicken pieces and cubed melon alternately onto the skewers.

Grill or Broil the Skewers:
- If using a grill, grill the skewers over medium-high heat for 8-10 minutes, turning occasionally, until the chicken is cooked through and nicely charred.
- If using a broiler, place the skewers on a foil-lined baking sheet and broil for 6-8 minutes, turning once halfway through cooking.

Glaze with Reserved Teriyaki Sauce:
- Brush the cooked skewers with the reserved teriyaki sauce during the last few minutes of grilling or broiling, allowing the sauce to caramelize slightly.

Serve and Garnish:
- Transfer the cooked melon teriyaki chicken skewers to a serving platter.
- Sprinkle with sesame seeds and sliced green onions for garnish, if desired.

Enjoy:
- Serve the melon teriyaki chicken skewers hot, accompanied by rice or a fresh salad.

Tips:

- Use ripe and sweet melon for the best flavor in this dish.
- Feel free to substitute chicken thighs or shrimp for the chicken breasts.
- If using wooden skewers, remember to soak them in water for at least 30 minutes before threading the ingredients to prevent burning on the grill.
- Customize the marinade by adding a splash of sriracha or chili flakes for a spicy kick.

These melon teriyaki chicken skewers are a perfect combination of sweet and savory flavors. They're great for outdoor grilling and make a delicious main course for any occasion. Enjoy!

Melon Coconut Rice Pudding

Ingredients:

- 1 cup Arborio rice (or any short-grain rice)
- 1 can (13.5 oz) coconut milk
- 2 cups water
- 1/4 teaspoon salt
- 1/4 cup granulated sugar (adjust to taste)
- 2 cups cubed ripe melon (cantaloupe, honeydew, or watermelon)
- 1/2 teaspoon vanilla extract
- Ground cinnamon, for garnish (optional)
- Toasted coconut flakes, for garnish (optional)

Instructions:

Cook the Rice:
- In a medium saucepan, combine the Arborio rice, coconut milk, water, and salt.
- Bring the mixture to a boil over medium-high heat, then reduce the heat to low.
- Cover and simmer gently for about 20-25 minutes, stirring occasionally, until the rice is tender and the mixture is creamy.

Add Sugar and Melon:
- Stir in the granulated sugar and cubed melon into the cooked rice pudding.
- Continue to cook for an additional 5-10 minutes over low heat, stirring occasionally, until the melon is softened and incorporated into the pudding.

Add Vanilla Extract:
- Remove the saucepan from the heat.
- Stir in the vanilla extract to enhance the flavor of the rice pudding.

Serve and Garnish:
- Spoon the melon coconut rice pudding into serving bowls.
- Garnish with a sprinkle of ground cinnamon and toasted coconut flakes, if desired.

Chill (Optional):
- For a chilled rice pudding, allow the pudding to cool slightly before covering and refrigerating until cold.

Enjoy:

- Serve the melon coconut rice pudding either warm or chilled, and enjoy this tropical and creamy dessert!

Tips:

- Use ripe and flavorful melons for the best taste in this dessert.
- Adjust the sweetness by adding more or less sugar according to your taste preference.
- Feel free to experiment with different types of melons or add other fruits such as diced pineapple or mango for additional tropical flavors.
- If you prefer a thicker pudding, cook the rice for a longer period of time until it reaches your desired consistency.
- This rice pudding can be served as a comforting dessert or a sweet breakfast treat.

This melon coconut rice pudding is a delicious and comforting dessert that's perfect for enjoying the flavors of summer. It's creamy, tropical, and sure to be a hit with family and friends. Serve it for a special occasion or simply as a delightful treat any time of the year!

Melon Margherita Pizza

Ingredients:

- 1 pre-made pizza dough (store-bought or homemade)
- Olive oil, for brushing
- 1 cup shredded mozzarella cheese
- 1 cup cherry or grape tomatoes, halved
- 1 cup cubed ripe melon (cantaloupe, honeydew, or watermelon)
- Fresh basil leaves, torn or chiffonade
- Balsamic glaze, for drizzling (optional)
- Salt and pepper, to taste

Instructions:

Preheat the Oven:
- Preheat your oven to the temperature specified for your pizza dough (usually around 450°F to 500°F / 230°C to 260°C).

Prepare the Pizza Dough:
- Roll out the pizza dough on a lightly floured surface into your desired shape (round or rectangular) to fit a pizza pan or baking sheet.

Assemble the Pizza:
- Place the rolled-out dough on a pizza pan or baking sheet lined with parchment paper.
- Lightly brush the dough with olive oil.

Add the Toppings:
- Sprinkle the shredded mozzarella cheese evenly over the pizza dough.
- Scatter the halved cherry or grape tomatoes on top of the cheese.
- Distribute the cubed melon pieces evenly across the pizza.

Season and Bake:
- Season the pizza with a pinch of salt and pepper, to taste.
- Place the pizza in the preheated oven and bake according to the dough instructions, usually for about 10-12 minutes or until the crust is golden and the cheese is bubbly and melted.

Finish and Garnish:
- Remove the pizza from the oven and let it cool slightly.
- Scatter torn or chiffonade fresh basil leaves over the hot pizza.
- Drizzle with balsamic glaze for added sweetness and flavor (optional).

Slice and Serve:

- Use a pizza cutter or sharp knife to slice the melon Margherita pizza into slices.
- Serve immediately and enjoy while warm!

Tips:

- Customize the pizza by adding additional toppings such as prosciutto slices, arugula, or a sprinkle of red pepper flakes for a touch of heat.
- Use your favorite melon variety for this pizza; each type brings a unique sweetness and flavor profile.
- If you prefer a crispier crust, you can pre-bake the pizza dough for a few minutes before adding the toppings.
- Experiment with different cheeses like fresh mozzarella or goat cheese for varied flavor experiences.

This melon Margherita pizza is a wonderful combination of savory, sweet, and fresh flavors. It's perfect for a light meal or appetizer, especially during the warmer months when melons are in season. Enjoy this creative pizza creation with family and friends!

Melon and Crab Salad

Ingredients:

- 1 cup cooked lump crab meat, chilled
- 2 cups cubed ripe melon (cantaloupe, honeydew, or watermelon)
- 1/4 cup red onion, thinly sliced
- 1/4 cup cucumber, diced
- 1/4 cup cherry tomatoes, halved
- 2 tablespoons fresh cilantro or parsley, chopped
- Juice of 1 lime
- 2 tablespoons extra-virgin olive oil
- Salt and pepper, to taste
- Optional: Mixed salad greens or arugula for serving

Instructions:

Prepare the Crab Meat:
- If using fresh crab meat, steam or boil the crab until cooked through. Allow it to cool, then pick the meat and chill it in the refrigerator. If using canned crab meat, drain and rinse it before chilling.

Prepare the Melon and Vegetables:
- Wash and cube the melon into bite-sized pieces.
- Thinly slice the red onion, dice the cucumber, and halve the cherry tomatoes.
- Chop the fresh cilantro or parsley.

Assemble the Salad:
- In a large mixing bowl, combine the chilled crab meat, cubed melon, sliced red onion, diced cucumber, cherry tomatoes, and chopped cilantro or parsley.

Make the Dressing:
- In a small bowl, whisk together the lime juice, extra-virgin olive oil, salt, and pepper to create the dressing.

Combine and Toss:
- Pour the dressing over the crab and melon mixture.
- Gently toss the salad ingredients together until well combined and evenly coated with the dressing.

Serve:
- Arrange the melon and crab salad on a serving platter or individual plates.
- Optionally, serve the salad over a bed of mixed salad greens or arugula.

Enjoy:
- Serve the melon and crab salad immediately and enjoy this refreshing and flavorful dish!

Tips:

- Choose ripe and sweet melons for the best flavor in this salad.
- Feel free to substitute the crab meat with cooked shrimp or lobster meat for variation.
- Add a touch of heat by adding a pinch of crushed red pepper flakes or finely diced jalapeño to the salad.
- This salad can be served as an appetizer, light lunch, or as part of a seafood-themed meal.

This melon and crab salad is perfect for summer gatherings or special occasions. It's light, colorful, and bursting with fresh flavors. Enjoy this delightful salad with family and friends!

Melon and Prosciutto Pasta

Ingredients:

- 8 ounces pasta of your choice (such as penne, fusilli, or linguine)
- 1 cup cubed ripe melon (cantaloupe, honeydew, or watermelon)
- 4 ounces thinly sliced prosciutto, cut into strips
- 1/4 cup chopped fresh basil leaves
- 1/4 cup grated Parmesan cheese, plus extra for serving
- 2 tablespoons extra virgin olive oil
- Salt and freshly ground black pepper, to taste
- Optional: Red pepper flakes, for a touch of heat

Instructions:

Cook the Pasta:
- Bring a large pot of salted water to a boil.
- Cook the pasta according to package instructions until al dente. Reserve about 1/2 cup of pasta cooking water, then drain the pasta.

Prepare the Ingredients:
- While the pasta is cooking, cube the melon, chop the fresh basil, and slice the prosciutto into strips.

Combine the Ingredients:
- In a large skillet or pan, heat the olive oil over medium heat.
- Add the prosciutto strips to the skillet and cook for 1-2 minutes until they start to crisp up slightly.

Add the Pasta and Melon:
- Add the cooked pasta to the skillet with the prosciutto.
- Toss to combine, adding a splash of reserved pasta cooking water if needed to loosen the pasta.

Incorporate Melon and Basil:
- Add the cubed melon and chopped basil to the skillet.
- Gently toss everything together until the melon is warmed through.

Season and Serve:
- Season the pasta with salt, freshly ground black pepper, and optional red pepper flakes to taste.
- Sprinkle grated Parmesan cheese over the pasta and toss again to combine.

Serve and Enjoy:
- Divide the melon and prosciutto pasta among serving plates or bowls.

- Garnish with additional grated Parmesan cheese and fresh basil leaves.
- Serve immediately and enjoy this delicious and unique pasta dish!

Tips:

- Choose ripe and flavorful melons for the best taste in this dish.
- If you prefer a creamier pasta, you can add a splash of heavy cream or pasta cooking water with melted butter to the skillet before tossing with the pasta.
- Customize the dish by using different types of pasta or adding additional ingredients like cherry tomatoes or baby spinach.
- Serve this melon and prosciutto pasta as a main course for a light summer dinner or as part of a pasta buffet for gatherings.

This melon and prosciutto pasta combines sweet, salty, and savory flavors into a satisfying meal that's quick and easy to prepare. Enjoy this flavorful pasta dish with family and friends!

Melon Panna Cotta

Ingredients:

- 2 cups cubed ripe melon (cantaloupe, honeydew, or watermelon)
- 1/4 cup water
- 1 packet (2 1/4 teaspoons) unflavored gelatin
- 1/2 cup granulated sugar
- 1 1/2 cups heavy cream
- 1/2 cup milk
- 1 teaspoon vanilla extract
- Mint leaves or additional melon, for garnish (optional)

Instructions:

Prepare the Melon Puree:
- In a blender or food processor, puree the cubed melon with water until smooth. You should have about 1 cup of melon puree. Set aside.

Bloom the Gelatin:
- In a small bowl, sprinkle the gelatin over 1/4 cup of cold water. Let it sit for about 5 minutes to soften and bloom.

Heat the Cream Mixture:
- In a saucepan, combine the heavy cream and sugar over medium heat. Stir until the sugar dissolves and the mixture is warm (but not boiling).

Add Gelatin and Melon Puree:
- Remove the cream mixture from the heat.
- Add the bloomed gelatin to the warm cream mixture, stirring until the gelatin is completely dissolved.
- Stir in the melon puree and vanilla extract until well combined.

Pour into Molds:
- Divide the melon panna cotta mixture evenly among serving glasses or molds.

Chill and Set:
- Place the filled glasses or molds in the refrigerator to chill and set for at least 4 hours, or until firm.

Serve and Garnish:
- Once set, remove the melon panna cotta from the refrigerator.
- Garnish with mint leaves or additional melon cubes, if desired.

Enjoy:

- Serve the melon panna cotta chilled and enjoy this creamy and refreshing dessert!

Tips:

- Use ripe and sweet melons for the best flavor in this dessert.
- Experiment with different varieties of melons to create unique flavor combinations.
- For a lighter version, you can use half-and-half or whole milk instead of heavy cream.
- If you prefer a smoother texture, strain the melon puree through a fine mesh sieve before adding it to the cream mixture.
- This melon panna cotta can be prepared ahead of time and kept in the refrigerator for up to 2-3 days before serving.

Melon panna cotta is a delightful dessert that's perfect for special occasions or anytime you want to impress with a creamy and fruity treat. Enjoy this elegant dessert with its delicate melon flavor!

Melon and Feta Bruschetta

Ingredients:

- 1 French baguette, sliced into 1/2-inch thick rounds
- 1 tablespoon olive oil
- 1 cup cubed ripe melon (cantaloupe, honeydew, or watermelon)
- 1/2 cup crumbled feta cheese
- 2 tablespoons fresh mint leaves, thinly sliced or torn
- Balsamic glaze, for drizzling (optional)
- Salt and black pepper, to taste

Instructions:

Prepare the Baguette Slices:
- Preheat the oven to 375°F (190°C).
- Arrange the baguette slices on a baking sheet.
- Brush both sides of the bread slices with olive oil.

Toast the Baguette Slices:
- Place the baking sheet in the preheated oven.
- Bake for about 8-10 minutes, flipping the slices halfway through, until the bread is golden and crispy.
- Remove from the oven and let the toasted baguette slices cool slightly.

Assemble the Bruschetta:
- In a mixing bowl, combine the cubed melon, crumbled feta cheese, and sliced mint leaves.
- Season with a pinch of salt and black pepper, to taste. Toss gently to combine.

Top the Baguette Slices:
- Spoon the melon and feta mixture evenly onto the toasted baguette slices.

Drizzle with Balsamic Glaze (Optional):
- If desired, drizzle a little balsamic glaze over each bruschetta for added flavor and presentation.

Serve and Enjoy:
- Arrange the melon and feta bruschetta on a serving platter.
- Serve immediately as a delicious and refreshing appetizer!

Tips:

- Choose ripe and flavorful melons for the best taste in this bruschetta.

- You can customize this recipe by adding a drizzle of honey or a sprinkle of red pepper flakes for a touch of sweetness or spice.
- Substitute fresh basil for the mint leaves if preferred.
- If you prefer a softer cheese, you can use goat cheese or ricotta instead of feta.
- This melon and feta bruschetta pairs well with a glass of chilled white wine or sparkling water.

Enjoy this melon and feta bruschetta as a delightful appetizer for parties, gatherings, or simply as a tasty snack. The combination of sweet melon, salty feta, and crunchy bread makes this dish a crowd-pleaser!

Melon and Mint Sorbet Float

Ingredients:

- 2 cups cubed ripe melon (cantaloupe, honeydew, or watermelon)
- 1/4 cup fresh mint leaves, plus extra for garnish
- 1/4 cup granulated sugar (adjust to taste)
- Juice of 1 lime
- 2 cups sparkling water or club soda, chilled
- Melon or mint sorbet (store-bought or homemade)
- Optional: Vodka or white rum (for an alcoholic version)

Instructions:

Prepare the Melon and Mint Mixture:
- In a blender or food processor, combine the cubed melon, fresh mint leaves, granulated sugar, and lime juice.
- Blend until smooth and well combined. Taste and adjust sweetness if needed by adding more sugar.

Strain (Optional):
- For a smoother sorbet base, strain the melon and mint mixture through a fine mesh sieve to remove any pulp or solids.

Chill the Mixture:
- Transfer the melon and mint mixture to a bowl or container.
- Cover and refrigerate until well chilled, about 1-2 hours.

Assemble the Floats:
- Fill glasses halfway with chilled sparkling water or club soda.

Add Sorbet and Melon Mint Mixture:
- Add a scoop of melon or mint sorbet into each glass of sparkling water.

Pour the Melon Mint Mixture:
- Pour the chilled melon and mint mixture over the sorbet in each glass, filling the glass almost to the top.

Garnish and Serve:
- Garnish each float with a sprig of fresh mint leaves.
- Optionally, add a splash of vodka or white rum to each float for an adult version.

Enjoy Immediately:
- Serve the melon and mint sorbet floats immediately with a straw and spoon to enjoy the refreshing combination of flavors and textures.

Tips:

- Choose ripe and flavorful melons for the best taste in this sorbet float.
- Customize the sorbet flavor by using melon sorbet, mint sorbet, or a combination of both.
- For an extra minty flavor, muddle fresh mint leaves with sugar in the bottom of each glass before adding the sparkling water and sorbet.
- This recipe can be easily doubled or tripled to serve a larger group.
- Serve these melon and mint sorbet floats at summer parties, BBQs, or as a special treat on hot days.

This melon and mint sorbet float is a refreshing and cooling dessert that's perfect for warm weather. Enjoy the combination of sweet melon, aromatic mint, and fizzy sparkling water in this delightful treat!

Melon Cucumber Rolls

Ingredients:

- 1 small cantaloupe or honeydew melon
- 1 large English cucumber
- 4 oz cream cheese, softened
- 2 tablespoons finely chopped fresh mint leaves
- Salt and black pepper, to taste
- Optional: Prosciutto or smoked salmon slices for wrapping

Instructions:

Prepare the Melon and Cucumber:
- Cut the cantaloupe or honeydew melon in half and scoop out the seeds.
- Use a melon baller or small spoon to scoop out melon balls from the flesh. Place the melon balls in a bowl and set aside.
- Wash the cucumber and trim the ends. Use a vegetable peeler to slice the cucumber lengthwise into thin, wide strips.

Mix the Cream Cheese Filling:
- In a small bowl, combine the softened cream cheese with the finely chopped fresh mint leaves. Season with salt and black pepper, to taste. Mix until well combined.

Assemble the Rolls:
- Lay a cucumber strip flat on a cutting board.
- Spread a thin layer of the cream cheese mixture evenly over the cucumber strip.
- Place a row of melon balls along one edge of the cucumber strip.

Roll Up the Cucumber:
- Carefully roll up the cucumber strip around the melon balls, starting from the edge with the melon.
- Secure the roll with a toothpick if needed. Repeat with the remaining cucumber strips and melon balls.

Optional: Add Prosciutto or Smoked Salmon:
- For added flavor and texture, you can wrap each cucumber roll with a slice of prosciutto or smoked salmon before rolling up the cucumber.

Chill and Serve:
- Arrange the melon cucumber rolls on a serving platter.
- Refrigerate for at least 30 minutes to chill and firm up before serving.

Garnish and Enjoy:

- Garnish the melon cucumber rolls with additional fresh mint leaves, if desired.
- Serve chilled and enjoy these delightful and refreshing bites!

Tips:

- Use a mandoline slicer to achieve uniform cucumber strips if preferred.
- Experiment with different variations by adding other ingredients such as avocado slices, shrimp, or crumbled feta cheese to the rolls.
- These melon cucumber rolls can be made ahead of time and stored in the refrigerator until ready to serve.
- Serve these rolls as an elegant appetizer for parties, brunches, or as a healthy snack.

Enjoy these melon cucumber rolls as a light and tasty treat that's perfect for summer entertaining or anytime you want a refreshing bite!

Melon and Pork Stir-Fry

Ingredients:

- 1 lb pork tenderloin or pork loin, thinly sliced
- 2 cups cubed ripe melon (cantaloupe, honeydew, or watermelon)
- 1 red bell pepper, thinly sliced
- 1 onion, thinly sliced
- 2 cloves garlic, minced
- 1-inch piece of ginger, minced
- 2 tablespoons soy sauce
- 1 tablespoon oyster sauce
- 1 tablespoon hoisin sauce
- 1 tablespoon rice vinegar
- 1 tablespoon cornstarch, dissolved in 2 tablespoons water
- 2 tablespoons vegetable oil
- Salt and pepper, to taste
- Cooked rice or noodles, for serving
- Chopped green onions or cilantro, for garnish (optional)

Instructions:

Prepare the Pork:
- Season the thinly sliced pork with salt and pepper.

Heat the Oil:
- Heat 1 tablespoon of vegetable oil in a large skillet or wok over medium-high heat.

Cook the Pork:
- Add the seasoned pork slices to the skillet and stir-fry for 3-4 minutes until browned and cooked through.
- Remove the cooked pork from the skillet and set aside.

Stir-Fry the Vegetables:
- In the same skillet, add another tablespoon of vegetable oil if needed.
- Add the sliced red bell pepper and onion to the skillet. Stir-fry for 2-3 minutes until the vegetables start to soften.

Add Garlic and Ginger:
- Add the minced garlic and ginger to the skillet. Stir-fry for 1 minute until fragrant.

Combine the Sauces:

- In a small bowl, mix together the soy sauce, oyster sauce, hoisin sauce, and rice vinegar.

Add Melon and Sauce:
- Add the cubed melon to the skillet with the cooked vegetables.
- Pour the sauce mixture over the vegetables and melon in the skillet.

Thicken the Sauce:
- Stir in the dissolved cornstarch mixture into the skillet.
- Cook for 1-2 minutes until the sauce thickens and coats the vegetables and melon.

Combine Pork and Serve:
- Return the cooked pork slices to the skillet.
- Stir everything together to combine and coat the pork, vegetables, and melon with the sauce.

Serve:
- Serve the melon and pork stir-fry hot over cooked rice or noodles.
- Garnish with chopped green onions or cilantro, if desired.

Tips:

- Choose ripe and flavorful melons for the best taste in this stir-fry.
- Adjust the sweetness and tanginess of the sauce to your preference by adding more or less hoisin sauce and rice vinegar.
- Feel free to add additional vegetables such as snow peas, broccoli, or snap peas to the stir-fry for extra color and texture.
- This melon and pork stir-fry is a delicious and satisfying meal that's perfect for a quick and flavorful dinner. Enjoy the sweet and savory combination of flavors!

Melon and Brie Quesadillas

Ingredients:

- 4 large flour tortillas
- 8 oz Brie cheese, thinly sliced
- 2 cups cubed ripe melon (cantaloupe, honeydew, or watermelon)
- 1 tablespoon honey
- Fresh basil leaves, torn or chopped
- Butter or olive oil, for cooking

Instructions:

Prepare the Ingredients:
- Slice the Brie cheese thinly.
- Cube the melon into bite-sized pieces.
- Tear or chop fresh basil leaves.

Assemble the Quesadillas:
- Lay out a flour tortilla on a clean surface.
- Arrange Brie cheese slices evenly over half of the tortilla.
- Spread cubed melon pieces over the Brie cheese.
- Drizzle a little honey over the melon.
- Sprinkle torn or chopped basil leaves on top.

Fold and Cook the Quesadillas:
- Fold the tortilla over to cover the filling, creating a half-moon shape.
- Repeat with the remaining tortillas and filling ingredients.

Cook the Quesadillas:
- Heat a large skillet or griddle over medium heat.
- Add a little butter or olive oil to the skillet.
- Place the filled quesadillas in the skillet and cook for 2-3 minutes on each side, or until golden brown and crispy, and the cheese is melted.

Serve and Enjoy:
- Remove the cooked quesadillas from the skillet.
- Let them cool slightly before cutting into wedges.
- Serve warm and enjoy these delicious melon and Brie quesadillas!

Tips:

- Use ripe and sweet melons for the best flavor in this quesadilla.

- Feel free to add a sprinkle of chili flakes or a dash of balsamic glaze for extra flavor.
- Experiment with different cheeses such as goat cheese or mozzarella if you prefer.
- Serve these quesadillas with a side of mixed greens or a simple tomato salad for a complete meal.

These melon and Brie quesadillas are a delightful fusion of flavors that will impress your family and friends. They make a great appetizer for parties or a quick and tasty meal any day of the week!

Melon and Blueberry Crisp

Ingredients:

For the Filling:

- 4 cups cubed ripe melon (cantaloupe, honeydew, or watermelon)
- 2 cups fresh blueberries
- 1/4 cup granulated sugar
- 2 tablespoons cornstarch
- 1 tablespoon lemon juice
- Zest of 1 lemon

For the Crisp Topping:

- 1 cup old-fashioned rolled oats
- 1/2 cup all-purpose flour
- 1/2 cup packed brown sugar
- 1/2 cup sliced almonds
- 1/2 teaspoon ground cinnamon
- 1/4 teaspoon salt
- 1/2 cup unsalted butter, melted

Instructions:

Preheat the Oven:
- Preheat your oven to 350°F (175°C). Grease a 9x9-inch baking dish or similar size with butter or cooking spray.

Prepare the Filling:
- In a large mixing bowl, combine the cubed melon and fresh blueberries.
- In a separate small bowl, mix together the granulated sugar, cornstarch, lemon juice, and lemon zest.
- Pour the sugar mixture over the melon and blueberries, and gently toss until well combined.

Make the Crisp Topping:
- In a medium bowl, combine the rolled oats, all-purpose flour, brown sugar, sliced almonds, ground cinnamon, and salt.
- Pour the melted butter over the oat mixture and stir until everything is evenly coated and crumbly.

Assemble and Bake:
- Transfer the melon and blueberry mixture into the prepared baking dish, spreading it out evenly.
- Sprinkle the crisp topping over the fruit mixture, covering it completely.

Bake the Crisp:
- Place the baking dish in the preheated oven and bake for 35-40 minutes, or until the fruit is bubbly and the topping is golden brown and crisp.

Serve and Enjoy:
- Remove the melon and blueberry crisp from the oven and let it cool slightly.
- Serve warm, optionally with a scoop of vanilla ice cream or whipped cream.

Tips:

- Feel free to use your favorite variety of melon for this crisp.
- Adjust the sweetness of the filling based on the sweetness of your melon and personal preference.
- You can substitute other fruits like peaches or raspberries for the blueberries, depending on availability and taste preference.
- Store any leftover crisp in an airtight container in the refrigerator and reheat before serving.

This melon and blueberry crisp is a wonderful summer dessert that showcases the best of seasonal fruits. The combination of sweet melon, tangy blueberries, and crunchy topping makes it a crowd-pleaser at any gathering or family dinner! Enjoy this delicious dessert warm with your favorite toppings.

Melon and Basil Lemonade

Ingredients:

- 4 cups cubed ripe melon (cantaloupe, honeydew, or watermelon)
- 1/2 cup fresh basil leaves, plus extra for garnish
- 1 cup freshly squeezed lemon juice (about 4-6 lemons)
- 1/2 cup granulated sugar (adjust to taste)
- 4 cups cold water
- Ice cubes, for serving

Instructions:

Prepare the Melon and Basil:
- In a blender or food processor, combine the cubed melon and fresh basil leaves.
- Blend until smooth and well combined.

Strain (Optional):
- If desired, strain the melon and basil mixture through a fine mesh sieve to remove any pulp or solids. This step is optional depending on your preference for texture.

Make the Lemonade Base:
- In a large pitcher, combine the freshly squeezed lemon juice and granulated sugar.
- Stir until the sugar is dissolved into the lemon juice.

Combine Melon Puree with Lemonade Base:
- Pour the melon and basil mixture into the pitcher with the lemonade base.
- Stir to combine.

Add Cold Water:
- Pour in the cold water and stir well to incorporate all ingredients.

Chill and Serve:
- Refrigerate the melon and basil lemonade until well chilled, about 1-2 hours.

Serve with Ice and Garnish:
- Fill glasses with ice cubes.
- Pour the chilled melon and basil lemonade into the glasses.
- Garnish each glass with a fresh basil leaf for an extra touch of flavor and presentation.

Enjoy:
- Stir the lemonade before serving to distribute the flavors.

- Serve and enjoy this refreshing melon and basil lemonade on a hot day!

Tips:

- Choose ripe and flavorful melons for the best taste in this lemonade.
- Adjust the sweetness of the lemonade by adding more or less sugar, depending on the sweetness of the melon and personal preference.
- For an extra herbal kick, muddle a few basil leaves with the sugar before combining with the lemon juice.
- Feel free to customize this recipe by adding sparkling water or a splash of vodka or gin for an adult version.
- This melon and basil lemonade is perfect for summer gatherings, picnics, or simply as a refreshing drink to enjoy anytime.

Enjoy this unique and flavorful melon and basil lemonade with family and friends. It's a delightful way to savor the flavors of summer!

Melon and Cilantro Rice

Ingredients:

- 1 cup long-grain white rice
- 2 cups water or vegetable broth
- 2 cups cubed ripe melon (cantaloupe, honeydew, or watermelon)
- 1/4 cup fresh cilantro, chopped
- 1 tablespoon lime juice
- Zest of 1 lime
- Salt, to taste
- Optional: Sliced green onions or chopped jalapeño for added flavor

Instructions:

Rinse and Cook the Rice:
- Rinse the rice under cold water until the water runs clear.
- In a saucepan, bring the water or vegetable broth to a boil.
- Add the rinsed rice to the boiling water, reduce the heat to low, cover, and simmer for 15-20 minutes, or until the rice is tender and the liquid is absorbed.

Prepare the Melon:
- While the rice is cooking, cube the ripe melon into bite-sized pieces.

Combine Ingredients:
- In a large mixing bowl, combine the cooked rice, cubed melon, chopped fresh cilantro, lime juice, and lime zest.
- Season with salt, to taste.

Add Optional Ingredients (if desired):
- For added flavor and texture, you can mix in sliced green onions or chopped jalapeño to the rice mixture.

Serve and Enjoy:
- Transfer the melon and cilantro rice to a serving dish.
- Serve warm as a side dish alongside grilled meats, seafood, or vegetables.

Tips:

- Use ripe and flavorful melons for the best taste in this rice dish.
- Adjust the amount of cilantro and lime juice based on your preference for flavor.
- Feel free to add other fresh herbs like mint or basil for additional freshness.
- This rice dish can be served warm or at room temperature.

- Leftover melon and cilantro rice can be stored in an airtight container in the refrigerator for a few days. Reheat gently before serving.

This melon and cilantro rice is a light and satisfying side dish that complements a variety of main courses. Enjoy the combination of sweet melon, zesty lime, and aromatic cilantro in this flavorful rice dish!

Melon and Ricotta Toast

Ingredients:

- Slices of your favorite bread (such as baguette, sourdough, or whole grain)
- 1 cup cubed ripe melon (cantaloupe, honeydew, or watermelon)
- 1/2 cup ricotta cheese
- Honey, for drizzling
- Fresh mint leaves, thinly sliced
- Optional: A sprinkle of sea salt or black pepper

Instructions:

Toast the Bread:
- Toast slices of bread until golden and crispy. You can use a toaster or toast them in the oven.

Prepare the Melon:
- Cube the ripe melon into bite-sized pieces.

Assemble the Toasts:
- Spread a generous layer of ricotta cheese on each slice of toasted bread.

Add the Melon:
- Arrange the cubed melon on top of the ricotta cheese.

Drizzle with Honey:
- Drizzle honey over the melon and ricotta. This adds a touch of sweetness to the toast.

Garnish:
- Sprinkle thinly sliced fresh mint leaves over the toast.

Optional: Season with Salt or Pepper:
- For a flavor contrast, you can sprinkle a little sea salt or black pepper over the toast. This is optional and depends on your taste preferences.

Serve and Enjoy:
- Serve the melon and ricotta toast immediately as a light breakfast, snack, or appetizer.

Tips:

- Use ripe and flavorful melons for the best taste in this toast.
- Experiment with different types of bread to suit your preference.
- Feel free to add other toppings such as a sprinkle of chopped nuts (like pistachios or almonds) or a drizzle of balsamic glaze for extra flavor.

- This toast can be customized based on what you have on hand. Try adding sliced strawberries or peaches along with the melon for a fruity variation.

Melon and ricotta toast is a delightful combination of creamy, sweet, and crunchy textures. It's quick to prepare and makes a satisfying and flavorful snack or light meal. Enjoy the fresh flavors of melon and ricotta cheese on toast!

Melon Breakfast Smoothie

Ingredients:

- 1 cup cubed ripe melon (cantaloupe, honeydew, or watermelon)
- 1 ripe banana, peeled and sliced
- 1/2 cup Greek yogurt (plain or vanilla)
- 1/2 cup almond milk or any milk of your choice
- 1 tablespoon honey or maple syrup (optional, adjust to taste)
- 1/2 teaspoon vanilla extract
- Ice cubes (optional, for a chilled smoothie)
- Fresh mint leaves or sliced strawberries, for garnish (optional)

Instructions:

Prepare the Ingredients:
- Cube the ripe melon and slice the banana.

Blend the Smoothie:
- In a blender, combine the cubed melon, sliced banana, Greek yogurt, almond milk, honey or maple syrup (if using), and vanilla extract.
- If you prefer a colder smoothie, add a handful of ice cubes to the blender.

Blend Until Smooth:
- Blend all the ingredients until smooth and creamy. If the smoothie is too thick, you can add more milk to reach your desired consistency.

Taste and Adjust:
- Taste the smoothie and adjust the sweetness by adding more honey or maple syrup if needed.

Serve and Garnish:
- Pour the melon breakfast smoothie into glasses.
- Garnish with fresh mint leaves or sliced strawberries for a decorative touch.

Enjoy Your Smoothie:
- Serve the melon breakfast smoothie immediately and enjoy as a nutritious and refreshing breakfast or snack!

Tips:

- Use ripe and flavorful melons for the best taste in this smoothie.
- Feel free to customize this smoothie by adding other fruits such as berries, peaches, or pineapple.

- Substitute the Greek yogurt with coconut yogurt or another dairy-free alternative for a vegan version.
- For added nutrition, you can blend in a handful of spinach or kale leaves for a green smoothie.
- This melon breakfast smoothie is versatile, so feel free to experiment with different ingredients and flavors to suit your taste preferences.

Start your day on a fresh note with this delicious and healthy melon breakfast smoothie.

It's packed with vitamins, minerals, and natural sweetness from the melon, making it a perfect way to fuel your morning!

Melon and Chicken Lettuce Wraps

Ingredients:

- 1 lb boneless, skinless chicken breasts, thinly sliced
- 2 cups cubed ripe melon (cantaloupe, honeydew, or watermelon)
- 1 red bell pepper, thinly sliced
- 1/2 cucumber, julienned
- 1 carrot, julienned
- 4-6 large lettuce leaves (such as butter lettuce, romaine, or iceberg)
- 2 tablespoons soy sauce
- 1 tablespoon hoisin sauce
- 1 tablespoon rice vinegar
- 1 tablespoon sesame oil
- 2 cloves garlic, minced
- 1-inch piece of ginger, grated
- Salt and pepper, to taste
- Sesame seeds and chopped green onions, for garnish
- Optional: Cooked rice noodles or vermicelli, for serving

Instructions:

Marinate the Chicken:
- In a bowl, combine the thinly sliced chicken with soy sauce, hoisin sauce, rice vinegar, minced garlic, grated ginger, sesame oil, salt, and pepper. Let it marinate for at least 15-20 minutes.

Cook the Chicken:
- Heat a large skillet or wok over medium-high heat.
- Add the marinated chicken slices and stir-fry for 5-6 minutes until cooked through and nicely browned.
- Remove the cooked chicken from the skillet and set aside.

Prepare the Vegetables and Melon:
- While the chicken is cooking, prepare the vegetables and melon.
- Cube the ripe melon and slice the red bell pepper, cucumber, and carrot into thin strips (julienne).

Assemble the Lettuce Wraps:
- Lay out the large lettuce leaves on a serving platter.
- Place a spoonful of cooked chicken onto each lettuce leaf.
- Top with cubed melon, sliced red bell pepper, julienned cucumber, and carrot.

Garnish and Serve:
- Sprinkle sesame seeds and chopped green onions over the lettuce wraps for garnish.
- Optionally, serve the lettuce wraps with cooked rice noodles or vermicelli on the side.

Wrap and Enjoy:
- To eat, fold the lettuce leaves around the filling like a taco or burrito.
- Enjoy these flavorful and refreshing melon and chicken lettuce wraps!

Tips:

- Use any variety of ripe melon for this recipe based on your preference.
- Feel free to add other vegetables like shredded cabbage, bean sprouts, or sliced snow peas to the lettuce wraps.
- Customize the sauce by adjusting the seasoning and adding chili sauce or Sriracha for a spicy kick.
- For a vegetarian version, substitute the chicken with tofu or cooked chickpeas.
- These lettuce wraps can be made ahead of time and stored in the refrigerator. Assemble just before serving for best results.

These melon and chicken lettuce wraps are perfect for a light lunch, appetizer, or healthy dinner option. They are packed with flavor and textures, making them a satisfying and enjoyable dish!

Melon Slaw

Ingredients:

- 3 cups cubed ripe melon (cantaloupe, honeydew, or watermelon)
- 1 cup shredded cabbage (green or purple)
- 1/2 cup shredded carrots
- 1/2 cup thinly sliced red onion
- 1/4 cup chopped fresh cilantro or mint leaves
- 1/4 cup chopped roasted peanuts or almonds (optional, for crunch)
- 1/4 cup mayonnaise or Greek yogurt
- 2 tablespoons apple cider vinegar or lime juice
- 1 tablespoon honey or maple syrup
- Salt and pepper, to taste

Instructions:

Prepare the Melon and Vegetables:
- Cube the ripe melon into bite-sized pieces.
- Shred the cabbage and carrots using a box grater or food processor.
- Thinly slice the red onion.

Combine the Salad Ingredients:
- In a large mixing bowl, combine the cubed melon, shredded cabbage, shredded carrots, sliced red onion, chopped cilantro or mint leaves, and chopped nuts (if using).

Make the Dressing:
- In a small bowl, whisk together the mayonnaise or Greek yogurt, apple cider vinegar or lime juice, honey or maple syrup, salt, and pepper until smooth and well combined.

Toss the Salad with Dressing:
- Pour the dressing over the melon and vegetable mixture in the bowl.
- Gently toss everything together until the salad is evenly coated with the dressing.

Chill and Serve:
- Cover the melon slaw and refrigerate for at least 30 minutes to allow the flavors to meld together.
- Serve the chilled melon slaw as a refreshing side dish or as a topping for grilled meats or sandwiches.

Tips:

- Use ripe and flavorful melons for the best taste in this slaw.
- Feel free to customize the vegetables based on what you have on hand. You can add sliced bell peppers, shredded broccoli, or snow peas for extra crunch and color.
- Substitute the mayonnaise with Greek yogurt for a lighter dressing option.
- Add a dash of hot sauce or crushed red pepper flakes for a spicy kick.
- This melon slaw can be made ahead of time and stored in the refrigerator for up to 2 days. Give it a quick toss before serving.

Enjoy this refreshing and colorful melon slaw as a side dish or light meal. It's perfect for summer gatherings, picnics, or any occasion where you want to showcase the sweetness of melon in a savory salad!

www.ingramcontent.com/pod-product-compliance
Lightning Source LLC
LaVergne TN
LVHW081558060526
838201LV00054B/1956